A Flashpoint in a MELTING POT

THE CROWN HEIGHTS RIOTS A WATERSHED FOR NEW YORK CITY

BRENDAN FINN
JOHN JAY COLLEGE OF CRIMINAL JUSTICE

Kendall Hunt
publishing company

On the cover: An overturned 88 Pct. RMP on the service road of Eastern Parkway is a metaphor for the Crown Heights Riots, because it started as an anti-Semitic riot and quickly turned into an anti-police riot. Ultimately, the rioters were expressing their anger and dissatisfaction with the dysfunctional government of New York City. As always, the police were merely the messenger, once again caught in the middle.

Cover image: © AP Photo/David Burns, File (9108210510)

Kendall Hunt
publishing company

www.kendallhunt.com
Send all inquiries to:
4050 Westmark Drive
Dubuque, IA 52004-1840

ISBN 978-0-7575-9840-1

Printed in the United States of America
10 9 8 7 6 5 4 3 2

Dedication

This book is dedicated to my wife, Patty, without whom it never would have happened. She is a person who makes dreams into reality, and has supported me on every level. Although, as you will see, I am rarely at a loss for words, I cannot begin to describe how important she was to this project. So I will simply say, "Thank you."

This is also dedicated to the men and women of the New York City Police Department who toiled for decades under the most adverse conditions. They always knew what to do and how to do it. It was the politics and the politicians that got in the way. Every honest, working cop (and that was almost all of us) who wore that shield should feel proud for being a part of a herculean effort. They told us in the Academy that it would be a thankless job, and they weren't lying. But it is amazing to look back at what the cops accomplished when given the right conditions. I am proud and humbled to say that I was a small part of it.

TABLE OF CONTENTS

Preface

The Crown Heights Riots

On a Saturday morning in late August 1991, I stood with other members of the NYPD Pipes and Drums, Bagpipe Band on a street corner in Bundoran, Donegal in the Republic of Ireland. We were waiting for the start of a parade that would wind through the streets of that tranquil beachfront town. As the band was preparing to strike up, a local fellow approached me and asked in his thick, northern Irish brogue, "So what do you think about those riots back home in Brooklyn?" You see, the Irish, especially the northern Irish, were cognizant of current events, especially in the "States." My friends and I were dumbfounded. None of us had heard anything about a riot, naturally, as we were vacationing and we hadn't been perusing the papers very diligently. Sensing that he now had an audience, the Irishman continued, "Yes, they've been rioting pretty good over there in Crown Heights, I think it is! So you have no idea what it's about?" And we didn't. But in time we would all come to find out all of the events of that bloody, tragic week in Crown Heights, Brooklyn, New York.

Soon enough, we would all be back in the US, back in New York and, for me, back in my old stomping grounds, the precinct where I began my career as a New York City police officer. The 71st Precinct, located on Empire Blvd. in Crown Heights, Brooklyn, has been the site of much controversy and more than a few "riot" situations. Crown Heights had also found itself at the center of many political and racial confrontations that continued to escalate from the 1970s through the late 1980s. By 1991 the neighborhood was ripe for the riot that indeed erupted, and it surprised no one. In fact, many political and social observers were wondering what took so long. For years the predictions of "a long hot summer" reverberated through the Police Department, especially among the rank-and-file, the cops on the street.

When I returned to work on August 28, the riots were more than a week in the past. But the Crown Heights, to which I returned, now resembled an armed camp. The army of occupation, the NYPD, was now stationed on every corner; wherever one turned, there was a cop. For years the black politicians and many of the liberal left had used the term "army of occupation" to characterize and describe the NYPD, because of the predominant amount of white cops from the suburbs. But now, the description had become reality. A sad reality.

Because I had been overseas during the actual event, I was forced to play catch up. The current newspapers, *The New York Times, The Daily News*, and *The Post* had already moved on. There were still stories concerning the event but they now had the tone of a historical narrative. Even my colleagues in the NYPD had put most of the sordid developments behind them and were now enjoying a respite from the violence. They were tired, and it took a lot of cajoling to get many of them to talk. Eventually, as with almost all cops, these events would emerge in what are called "war stories," but by that time the events would also be the equivalent of yesterday's news, ancient history in this media-obsessed nation.

I would eventually find out what happened, but it would be a long journey.

As the residents of Crown Heights and the people of New York City attempted to put those tragic events behind them, it became obvious that there would be a great deal of political and social upheaval. After all, that is what a riot is. Typically in the wake of such cataclysmic events there is a great deal of finger-pointing, second-guessing, and "Monday morning quarter- backing." This riot would be no different. What was different was the nature of the conflagration and the reasons behind it; including how it was allowed to develop, and the root causes. Then there would be the questions pertaining to the response by the police and the city. Instantly the howls of protest and outrage arose from many corners of the political landscape. And there were many valid claims as well as bona fide victims with legitimate issues.

As the victims and the targets of the violence during the riot, the Hasidic community of Crown Heights angrily wanted to know—they had a right to know—what happened to police protection. For the better part of four days they were prisoners in their own homes, hoping and waiting for the NYPD to step in and restore law and order to their community. In the politically charged language of that era, the Jewish Hasidim claimed to be the victims of a "pogrom," a term revived from the days of the Crusades, Eastern Europe, Nazi Germany, and the Holocaust. A pogrom describes religious persecution and, as far as the Hasidic community was concerned, that is what happened. Pogrom or not, there was ample evidence and a great deal of anecdotal information that indicated this was a war between the Blacks and the Jews of Crown Heights. That is not to say that the black community of Crown Heights, the Caribbean immigrants, their progeny, and the African-Americans did not have their own legitimate issues. Although there are no issues that validate the taking of another person's life or the destruction of property, the Blacks of Crown Heights were long suffering in their own minds and in the minds of many observers.

War or merely a riot, this event brought to light, for everyone to see, just how far out of control the simmering animosity and antagonism had gone. It was no longer below the surface. It had simmered, bubbled, and boiled over. What happened in Crown Heights was a Flashpoint in a Melting Pot!

I was not present for the riots but my previous experience in Crown Heights, working as a rookie cop in the 71st Precinct in 1984, piqued my interest in the event and provided a solid if not unique historical perspective. You see, it is the men and the women of the NYPD who stand in the middle of the two interest groups, people who on the surface may seem diametrically opposed but a closer look reveals more similarities and commonalities than either might care to admit.

My very first day on patrol as a New York City police officer was an education and an eye-opener. As I walked out to my post in my stiff, new uniform down Empire Boulevard past Nostrand Avenue and on to Rogers Avenue, I felt like a tourist in a foreign country. Actually I felt like a tourist passing through many foreign countries in a short time. First there was the Eglise de Dieu, with scores of Haitian women donning white turbans, the men wearing white robes. I knew it was some sort of a Catholic church, but nothing I had seen before. In no time I was in front of "Gloria's In and Out," a Jamaican restaurant featuring roti, a Caribbean dish I had never heard of or seen. The smell of curry was in the air and this young, inexperienced policeman knew then and there that it would be a learning experience. In a few more minutes the classroom included a couple of Rastafarian men with their dreadlocks piled high above their head in a cone-shaped device. The hair went about four to five feet in the air. It was startling. In what must have been a foreign tongue these men were yelling to me, as I gaped at them, that the traffic light was broken. It took me awhile to understand the version of English they were speaking, but it was indeed English. And they were right, the light was broken and I started to direct traffic.

Later on, just when I thought the foreign studies lesson had ended, I reached Eastern Parkway and bumped into a group of men in long dark coats, broad-brimmed hats, and curly hair that gave way to fairly long beards. These men were walking fast with some women trailing behind. The women were dressed in what appeared to be very fashionable, expensive dresses. The young boys, dressed like little men, were further back, obviously emulating their dads. I would later find that these were Lubavitcher Hasidim, and their world headquarters was located right here on Eastern Parkway. Their synagogue, known by its address as 770 Eastern Parkway, was an impressive three-story building with a collegiate style of architecture, somewhat Gothic but parochial. This building might fit in at my old alma mater, Fordham University. It felt like a place of learning and a place of worship. 770 Eastern Parkway was the center of the Lubavitcher world and the epicenter of these Hasidic people here in Crown Heights.

Down Kingston Avenue I walked, trying to get the feel of my new precinct. Shop after shop offered signs written in Hebrew. Hundreds of Lubavitchers hurried up and down the street. Kingston Avenue was their shopping and mercantile district. Another turn onto President Street revealed imposing brownstones and mansions out of Town and Country magazine. The houses were beautiful and old and smelled of "old money." The lawns were immaculate and immense with great evergreen trees and shrubs decorating the landscape. I later found out that many of these were inhabited by Lubavitcher families, but just as many were owned by black families, many of them doctors who had been residing here for decades. Later on, a veteran cop would point out where former congresswoman Shirley Chisholm lived. It was indeed a mansion.

Finally I traversed to another end of the precinct, closer to Flatbush Avenue, which was the western terminus of the 71st. Here was another group of people, mostly American Blacks but also some Hispanics. They were living in older, rundown apartment buildings, some with overflowing garbage problems. Kids ran through the dangerous streets avoiding the cars that streamed through the area. A closer look revealed that this area was once a vaunted neighborhood of Brooklyn. The Brooklyn Dodgers had played a block away on the corner of Bedford Ave and McKeever Place. There were two testaments to that storied past, the Ebbets Field Houses, a huge complex of apartment buildings located on the hallowed ground previously patrolled by Duke Snyder and Gil Hodges, and a block away was Jackie Robinson Junior High School. A fitting homage to the man who had broken the color barrier in Major League Baseball and now served as an inspiration to all the peoples of this precinct as they attempted to navigate the troubled waters of Brooklyn and America. Yes, I had walked into the proverbial melting pot. My early career would be a crash course in immigrants, immigration, and cultural conflict. My job would reveal itself to be that of a street-side arbiter, a referee settling disputes, sometimes between people who spoke two different languages, neither of them English. Sometimes the people spoke the same language but didn't want to understand each other. That turned out to be a big problem here. I would also come to find that these problems I was encountering as a rookie street cop were magnified and multiplied to almost geometric proportions on higher levels. The commanding officer of the 71st needed to be one part cop, one part arbitrator, one part soothsayer, and one part magician, the magic being the most important part, because only a magician could pull off this balancing act. As we later found out, the 71st Precinct was more than a melting pot; it was a powder keg waiting to explode. Crown Heights itself was that simmering melting pot. For many of those in charge, it was actually a pressure cooker.

The precinct commander was always under pressure from the upper echelon of the NYPD and the mayor's office. He needed to keep the neighborhood calm. This was not an easy job, because the two major ethnic/racial groups were at odds with each other. There was a perception that the Hasidim had significant influence with the precinct commander and, for that matter, with the mayor. This perception frustrated and annoyed the black residents of Crown Heights. Sometimes these frustrations would boil over and there would be protests, sometimes skirmishes with Hasidim, sometimes with police. Sometimes the Hasidim skirmished with the police also. Yes, the precinct commander walked a tightrope. Yet, having the 71st precinct commander post in your résumé was obviously a bonus, as the former chief of department had once been the precinct commander, and now the current police commissioner, Raymond Kelly, also had commanded the 71st. If you navigated the tricky, treacherous political waters of Crown Heights, there was a reward waiting on the other side. If you didn't, most likely a promising police career would be in jeopardy.

Because of this fact of life, every decision in the 71st, even the little ones, were made with excruciating calculation as to the effect on the community. At any moment even the smallest, most innocuous-seeming incident could spin out of control. Every protest was carefully prepared for by the NYPD staff. The NYPD was cognizant of the importance of Crown Heights. Since Crown Heights was the home of two important constituencies of the Democratic Party, City Hall was also conscious of the neighborhood. It was a well-known fact of political life in the city that the Hasidic people voted in a bloc and for the candidate whom the rebbe endorsed. It was of paramount political importance to keep these people and the rebbe happy. On the other hand, the American and Caribbean Blacks also represented an important voting bloc for a Democratic candidate; in fact, the Democratic leader of Brooklyn was a black man from Crown Heights, Clarence Norman Jr. Immigrants and Blacks were also significant, stalwart interest groups of the party. Yes, Crown Heights was a political minefield, and City Hall made sure that the precinct commander understood the importance of not stepping on any mines; the importance of peace and tranquility in the neighborhood was at stake.

The activists also understood the political significance of Crown Heights. Realizing that the issues in the neighborhood were a microcosm of racial and ethnic politics, many of these activists used Crown Heights as stage, as political theater to dramatize their racial and political issues. As a result, the area was the scene of many political protests, called "Days of Outrage." It seemed that Crown Heights embodied many of the issues that were important to the black activists who emerged in the mid 1980s: Al Sharpton, Herbert Daughtry, and Sonny Carson, three of the more high-profile men of that era, and many other lower-profile but equally determined and perhaps even more committed to the cause. Some of these activists had been looking for a place to air their grievances, to draw attention to their issues. Some of these activists believed in the "politics of confrontation." They wanted controversy, and if it came to violence, so be it. Some of these activists had ties to the Black Liberation Army and were throwbacks to the protests of the 1960s. For them, Crown Heights presented the opportunity to expose the injustices of New York City and of America. There was a perception within the community at large that some of these groups may have been looking for a battleground in the ongoing class struggle.

After my time in the 71st Precinct ended, I moved my way through a career path in the Police Department, but always remembered where I came from. Because the other half of the 71st Precinct was a high-crime area, the cops in the precinct were a tight, close-knit group. Long after leaving the precinct, cops would return to socialize with the former partners and workmates, and 71 alumni watched with special interest when something was going on in "the Heights," because they knew just how delicate the situation could be. As a matter of fact, one of the units I worked with after my transfer from the 71st was the Brooklyn South Task Force. As one may surmise from the name of the unit, this group was responsible for policing major events and responding to violent or controversial situations, sometimes even riots.

For that reason, the commanding officer and many of the cops from the Brooklyn South Task Force spent a lot of time in Crown Heights. There were always protests going on and the neighborhood required special attention. I also had a lot of friends in the task force; in fact, my sister also worked there for many years as a police officer. So, as many people do, I kept track of my old stomping grounds long after I left. When I heard the news of the riot, even though I was standing on a street corner in Ireland, I was concerned for my sister, my friends, and for the people of Crown Heights.

The following pages represent a journey of sorts through Crown Heights, the people who live there, the problems they deal with, and their attempts to solve those problems. But the story also documents a journey for those people, who come from diverse geographical, racial, and ethnic backgrounds. For many of them it is a tale of immigration, landing in America, and trying to start a better life. For many more it is a tragic story of slavery and bondage, being transported to the New World against their will. Both groups have endured hardships and have survived. It is also a story of policing in a city and in a neighborhood where crime had taken over, and where simple misunderstandings can explode into violent situations. This is the story of Crown Heights.

CHAPTER 1
A HOT SUMMER NIGHT IN BROOKLYN

On a hot Monday night, August 20, 1991, a motorcade of Lubavitcher Hasidic Jews was traveling through the streets of Crown Heights, returning to the President Street home of the Grand Rebbe, Menachem Schneerson. The motorcade was led, as usual, by an NYPD 71st Precinct radio car. As the motorcade drove through the intersection of President Street and Utica Avenue, the last car, driven by Josef Lifsch slammed into a car traveling northbound on Utica Avenue. Lifsch's station wagon careened out of control and onto the sidewalk of President Street. Eight-year-old Gavin Cato and his six-year-old cousin, Angela, had been riding their bikes on the sidewalk when Lifsch's car slammed into them, killing Gavin and seriously injuring Angela.

The next four days were some of the most violent and racially charged periods in New York City since the dramatic confrontations of the late 1960s. These were racially and ethnically motivated, but the perception was that this violence, this riot, was an anti-Semitic riot. It was the Blacks against the Jews. The police were in the middle but also were the objects of the crowd's ire. The violence that started on Monday night was not brought under control until early Friday morning. Neighborhood stores had been burned and many residents, mostly Jewish, had been cowering as prisoners in their own homes. The media and the Jewish community were irate. They asked: How could this riot be allowed to rage out of control for so long? Why didn't Mayor Dinkins do something about it sooner? Why did the police stand back and let things rage out of control?

The questions were often answered by the same people who posed them—the Jewish community and the media. And the answer in many of their minds was that David Dinkins, the city's first African-American mayor, had allowed the crowd to vent, instructing the police to use restraint and allow the crowd to get its frustrations out. These were charges that most likely would never be proven, but they were leveled nonetheless.

In the aftermath of the riot, a commission was empanelled to investigate the riot and the response. The commission undertook a lengthy and extensive investigation. The report was released in two volumes and had all the appearances of being comprehensive. When all was said and done, the commission affixed the ultimate blame on the mayor for not ensuring that the police department did its job. The criticism for the police department was decidedly less muted. The field commanders and chiefs were roundly blamed for what was apparent incompetence and lack of preparation. The language may not have been as blatant, but the report made it no secret that the police were to blame. As the ultimate boss, the mayor took blame also. But he was also credited with correcting the problem, righting the foundering police department ship, and telling his commissioner that changes had to be implemented.

What the commission would not address, what nobody in government wanted to admit was that it was government, the Democratic Party in particular, that was to blame for the mess of Crown Heights. The Crown Heights riot was, in the words of the *New York Times*, "two underdogs colliding," describing the combatants in the riot, the Blacks and the Jews. But the Crown Heights Riot was also a flashpoint in a melting pot that had been simmering for a long time, and the accident and the response to that accident are what set off the black community.

How could a tragic, seemingly accidental incident like that set off a community? The answer is as complicated as it is obvious. For too many years the black community of Crown Heights seethed over the perception, real or not, that the Lubavitcher community had been the recipient of unconcealed political patronage and favoritism. The black community was angry and envious of what they perceived were injustices against them by the government of New York City. And the government of New York City was run by the Democratic Party.

What developed were two special interest groups of the Democratic Party fighting each other for control of a neighborhood, with the black community resenting the fact that a 15 percent minority population was controlling their community. True or not, we know that perception can often overrule reality. In the case of Crown Heights, there is much evidence and anecdotal information that indicate that the perception was indeed the reality.

For more than three decades New York City was mismanaged by the Democratic Party, at times to the brink of financial collapse. But the neglect and mismanagement of Crown Heights epitomized the depth of the problem until finally a spark ignited a riot in that community. The result was a realignment in New York City politics. That the Democratic Party failed was obvious to the Hasidic community in Crown Heights, but it must have also been apparent to the black community that rioted against the Jews and against the police, which, in effect, represented New York City government and the Democratic Party.

But the rioters in Crown Heights weren't necessarily the residents of the community, and that group did not represent a cross-section of the black community. The black community of Crown Heights was and is composed of two groups of black people: American Blacks and Caribbean Blacks. The Caribbean black group comprises a larger percentage of the population than the American black group, which has been residing in the area since the early days of Brooklyn. Both of these groups arrived in Crown Heights either as refugees from another country or another part of New York City. They arrived in Crown Heights and in Brooklyn searching for their version of the American Dream.

The Lubavitcher Hasidic Jews comprise a small percentage of the Crown Heights population, close to 15 percent. But they have held enormous clout in the community and in New York City for many years, mostly because they can mobilize voters and almost guarantee elections. They also arrived in this country as refugees, once again seeking another version of the American Dream, which differs greatly from that of the Caribbean and African arrivals. The Lubavitchers came to Crown Heights to revive their religious community and establish a worldwide headquarters, which is now on Eastern Parkway.

These three groups have found themselves living side-by-side in Crown Heights, one of the older communities in Brooklyn that was probably founded by Blacks in the early nineteenth century. They supplanted the Irish, Italian, German, and Jewish immigrants who had previously dominated the area. Crown Heights is a true melting pot with all the problems that accompany divergent cultures trying to coexist or merely trying to exist.

This story traces the origins of these groups; explains their individual cultural experiences, experiences that define their collective group personality. All three of these groups are, as stated above, stalwarts of the Democratic Party, each attempting to grab their share of the proverbial pie. The Democratic Party and New York City government let each of these groups down. The American and Caribbean Blacks grew increasingly disenfranchised by the political patronage that was made available to the Lubavitchers. The riot was one manifestation of that frustration and disenchantment. The Lubavitchers felt betrayed when they were cowering in their own homes while unruly, violent mobs rampaged through their streets shouting anti-Semitic slurs and assaulting members of the Lubavitcher community. It was the job of New York City's government to protect them and it failed badly.

Exacerbating the problem is the history of the black people, whether Caribbean or African in descent. Their history, of slavery here and in the Caribbean, is one of the great tragedies of history. The Lubavitcher and Jewish history of facing discrimination and persecution is equally compelling. That these three groups should find themselves at odds with each other on the streets of New York is just one more sad chapter in their history. But it is an American story just as the Civil Rights Movement is an important component of African-American history. The lessons of the Civil Rights Movement and some of the methods were also employed in Crown Heights by a group of activists who used Crown Heights as a battlefield in their ongoing war against what they call white oppression. One of their slogans was "No Justice, No Peace!" and Crown Heights is evidence that they meant every word.

Crown Heights became a battleground because of mismanagement by the Democratic Party, because it did not arrange some sort of compromise in the community and because there were outside forces at work, the black activists, who recognized that this was an area that represented what was wrong in New York City. Caught in the middle, as usual, were the men and women of the New York City police department, who naturally were not blameless in the situation, but were, for the most part, the pawns of New York City government. In the end, it was the NYPD that received the lion's share of blame in the riot, from a commission that seemed to time its conclusions with the impending mayoral election.

But the results of that mayoral election, the triumph of a Republican candidate, Rudy Giuliani, over the incumbent, David Dinkins, is the telltale fact that the riot had indeed affected New York City politics. The continuing domination of the Republican Party, now in its 18th year, is just one more reminder of the dissatisfaction with the Democratic Party by city residents. That a profoundly Democratic city continues to reelect a Republican mayor is, perhaps, one of those urban legends that is hard to believe. But it is true.

The accident that evening was a flashpoint in a melting pot. The early riot that ensued was a primal scream from a community, mostly Caribbean Blacks, who were frustrated. The ensuing days were a manifestation of the politics of confrontation that reached their fruition in riots. The end result was that the Democratic Party lost a stalwart group of voters, who reached across the divide and voted Republican the next time. Although Crown Heights was a loser during that tumultuous week in August, the end result may have changed New York City in the long run.

This is the story of the build-up to the riot; the history of the peoples who came to live in Crown Heights and the place itself. It is not a blow-by-blow account of the riot because that has been covered in the Girgenti Commission Report. It is a short history of corruption in New York City politics and how that corruption allowed a problem in a community to fester. The Democratic Party leaders mismanaged the finances of New York City, and the city almost went bankrupt. During that period, either through misguided political ideas or through mismanagement, the Democratic Party allowed crime to proliferate to the point that the city was unsafe. The fiscal crisis and rising crime created an untenable situation in the city, especially in the poorer communities. The police department was both mismanaged and hamstrung by politics, and this created a culture of passivity that allowed the situation to explode in Crown Heights.

Once again, it was a flashpoint in a melting pot.

CHAPTER 2 BROOKLYN: THE CITY OF CHURCHES; THE BOROUGH OF STRUGGLE.

"In Brooklyn I never felt myself a minority for everyone there was a minority."
– Miriam Gottdank Isaacs.[1]

Driving over the Brooklyn Bridge from Manhattan, the sign announces: "Welcome to Brooklyn, America's Fourth Largest City." In the shadow of Manhattan, the Borough of Brooklyn is indeed larger than all but three American cities, but it is itself no longer a city, having been annexed by New York City in 1898, a development long ago foreshadowed by a citizens group lamenting in advance the loss of Brooklyn's character.[2] Though no longer a city in its own right, Brooklyn never lost its character. It continues to be a destination for immigrants and a place where people struggle to create their own American Dream.

Brooklyn has always had its share of controversy, from its earliest incarnation as a Dutch village in 1636, part of the larger colony called New Amsterdam. Its moniker, City of Churches, harkens from those early days and the plethora of churches dotting its landscape, including the Dutch Reform Church, which still sits at the intersection of Church Avenue and Flatbush Avenue. From the inception it was a place inhabited by a broad demographic, including Blacks and Jews. When New Amsterdam governor Kieft granted Anthony Jansen Van Salee, a former African pirate, 200 acres in Kings County, the history of black people in Brooklyn began.[3] It would become an illustrious, yet controversial history.

In the summer of 1664 a British fleet sailed into what would later become New York harbor, effectively settling an ongoing battle between the Dutch and the English. "The province was settled without bloodshed and the government of the colony passed into English hands."[4] It was only one of many struggles in the long history of this borough.

New Amsterdam was already a thriving commercial and transportation hub, while the village of Brooklyn and the six towns of Kings Country were initially rural. Most of these towns—New Utrecht, Gravesend, Flatlands, Flatbush, Brooklyn, and Bushwick—bear the Anglicized names from the original Dutch. For example, Brooklyn was spelled Bruckelen, and Bushwick was spelled Boswyc. These six towns are still major neighborhoods in the borough of Brooklyn.

In 1660 the first "free black," Francisco de Negar, was among 23 petitioners for land patents in Bushwick.[5] By this time it was established that there were not only free black men in the Long Island villages that made up Kings County, but also many African slaves.[6] Slavery was deemed necessary by the Dutch West India Company in its commercial endeavors, and was continued by the British after the takeover of the colony.

The village of Brooklyn, closest in proximity to Manhattan, became a thriving commercial entity in its own right. As more people came to live on that side of the river, the boundaries continued to push east- and southward. Soon the Lefferts family would own and settle the town of Bedford. In the mid 1700s this area was mainly farmland with some major roads passing through it. One of those roads was the Kings Highway, a well-traveled route connecting the towns of Flatbush and Brooklyn.[7]

Immediately to the east of Bedford was a developing black community named after one of its founders, James Weeks. Beginning in 1838 the area called Weeksville-Carrville was purchased from the John Lefferts' estate by Henry C. Thompson, who sold 32 plots to Weeks, who would subdivide and sell them to other Blacks. This would eventually become the modern day neighborhood known as Bedford-Stuyvesant, one of the leading centers of black culture in the twentieth century.

A ridge road formed the southern boundary of this area, running eastward from Prospect Heights toward Brownsville and then Queens. This well-traveled route would become the grand Eastern Parkway, intersecting the area known as Crow Hill, named for the tallest hill, whose trees were frequented by many crows that were reported to fly over the area on their way to a nesting area in Jamaica.[8] Part of the town of Bedford, Crow Hill was early settled by manumitted black slaves and later saw the arrival of working-class immigrant families: Irish, German, and Jews.[9] In its early history, however, Crow Hill was a neighborhood on the fringe and beyond the pale. According to many newspaper accounts from this early period, it seemed to have the feel of a western town, complete with drinking and gambling establishments and the ubiquitous problems that invariably accompany them. By the early 1900s Crow Hill would be called Crown Heights.[10]

Through the 1800s the village of Brooklyn continuously acquired the surrounding towns until Kings County was known as Brooklyn. By the time it was annexed by New York, Brooklyn had undergone a remarkable transformation from a rural village to a commercial hub. These changes affected the outlying areas such as Crow Hill, which had seen its own changes in demographics, from a primarily black community to the above-mentioned immigrant groups of Irish, Germans, and Jews. With the completion of Eastern Parkway and Crown Street, that transformation took the name of Crown Heights. The black residents were pushed toward the neighboring towns of Weeksville-Carrville and Bedford-Stuyvesant.

As the spigot of immigration continued to flow virtually undiminished, the influx of these newer immigrant groups had an almost drowning effect on the black population of Brooklyn. Harold X. Connolly explained this phenomenon in *A Ghetto Grows in Brooklyn:* "As a result of this enormous increase in Whites, the actual proportion of blacks in the total Brooklyn population declined precipitously from 27 percent in 1800 to 4.6 percent in 1840 and to less than 2 percent in 1860. Not until 1930 did this percentage again exceed 2 percent."[11]

The tremendous population and demographic shifts did not end in the 1930s however. The Crown Heights neighborhood that became an entrenched Irish/German/Jewish neighborhood would eventually see an incredibly large influx of American Blacks from the South and West Indian Blacks in what has come to be called the Great Migration of the late 1950s and on into the 1970s. During that period many communities in Brooklyn and elsewhere in New York City experienced tremendous swings in ethnic and racial demographics. As a result of this Great Migration from the South, Central Brooklyn was beginning to overflow.[12] By 1964 Crown Heights was a neighborhood undergoing profound changes.

CHAPTER 3

BLACKS AND JEWS COME TO BROOKLYN

"HOW SHALL WE SING THE LORD'S SONG IN A STRANGE LAND?"
PSALM 137:4

The year 1964 was one of tremendous change in America. The assassination of President John F. Kennedy in late 1963 was a shocking moment in American history, and perhaps the end of innocence for many Americans. The increased tensions of the Cold War, the dramatic scenes of the Civil Rights Movement, and the entrance of the Vietnam War into the American living room via television all contributed to the changing American landscape, both physically and figuratively.

Crown Heights and Brooklyn were experiencing their own profound changes along with America. The Great Migration of rural southern Blacks northward was flooding the neighborhoods of Brooklyn, particularly Bedford-Stuyvesant, Brownsville, and Crown Heights.[1] Coupled with a huge migration of West Indian blacks from the Caribbean Islands, the demographic was changing dramatically. [2]

Throughout the 1930s, 40s, and 50s, Crown Heights had been the bastion of immigrant working-class people hailing primarily from Europe. The Irish, Germans, and Jews had discovered Crown Heights as a neighborhood with newly constructed, affordable housing and embraced the area. The high-rise apartment buildings on Eastern Parkway and in the surrounding area were the symbol of affluence for this neighborhood and marked a comfortable lifestyle.

When the Brooklyn Dodgers announced in 1955 that they were forsaking their Bedford Avenue address for the greener pastures of Los Angeles, the handwriting was on the wall for Crown Heights and, for that matter, much of central Brooklyn.[3] The inevitable decay of housing and the increasing movement of people to the suburbs started a demographic shift in Crown Heights that began as a trickle but by 1964 ended in a tidal wave.

As the Dodgers were heading west, many of the Whites in Crown Heights were heading east, to other neighborhoods of Brooklyn and Queens and even farther out on Long Island. This phenomenon, called White Flight, was new to New York City, where the old European ethnic groups had ruled their neighborhoods for decades, but now the flood of black immigrants from points south had pushed them to new neighborhoods.[4]

People from the Caribbean had been immigrating to the United States for centuries in what has been described as three waves. The third wave of Caribbean immigration came in the mid 1960s during the immigration reform of the Lyndon Johnson era.[5] The people of the Islands, particularly Jamaica, Trinidad, and Haiti, started arriving in the neighborhoods of central Brooklyn. As central Brooklyn became flooded with people, the overflow spilled out to Crown Heights, Bushwick, East New York, and Brownsville.[6]

The most vivid evidence of this new migration came marching down Eastern Parkway on Labor Day in 1967 as the first Carnival Parade of West Indians in the colorful costumes of their native islands.[7] While the Caribbeans were celebrating on the streets of Crown Heights, the Irish and Germans were leaving their beloved Ninth Ward and moving to Marine Park, Canarsie, the Rockaways, and Breezy Point. But one Crown Heights ethnic group was not joining the White Flight. That group was the Lubavitcher Hasidim.

By the time Joseph Schneerson arrived in Crown Heights in 1940, black people had been living in Brooklyn for almost 300 years. Some of the earliest settlements had been established by free blacks, and the neighborhoods had historically been black since the early 1800s. By the time of the Draft Riots of 1864, Crown Heights featured a significant black population that swelled, as refugees from the Manhattan violence journeyed to safety in that area.[8]

As we have seen, the three-decade period of European immigration changed that demographic for nearly a century, but by 1964 a major reversal was underway. In *A Covenant with Color*, Craig Steven Wilder describes this as the "expanding Brooklyn Ghetto," which grew out of Bedford-Stuyvesant. During the period from 1940 to 1990, Kings County had a net loss of 1.5 million white residents and a net gain of 1.3 million black residents in this White Flight phenomenon.[9]

As the majority of Whites streamed out of Crown Heights in the early 1960s, Menachem Schneerson, the grand rebbe of the Lubavitchers, was faced with a difficult decision: whether to remain in their enclave with its epicenter at 770 Eastern Parkway or join the other Whites in exodus. There were complex factors weighing into the decision, not the least of which was the nomadic journey the Lubavitchers had undertaken to arrive in Crown Heights.

The Long Journey of the Lubavitcher Hasidim

In 1940 Poland, Hitler and the Wermacht were approaching. As the Germans loomed ominously, so did a sense of dread for Joseph Schneerson, the Lubavitcher rebbe in the city of Warsaw. The sense of dread was part fear of what havoc and death the Germans might inflict, but also a dread of making a difficult, life-changing decision: to stay in his homeland of Poland or to emigrate to the safety of America. His people needed him in Poland but the Lubavitcher mission might be better served by his leaving. Schneerson agonized over the decision but acquiesced to some sensible advisors. He arrived in New York City in late 1940 and joined a small but dedicated group of Lubavitcher Hasidim in Crown Heights, Brooklyn. This small settlement had been brought out to Crown Heights by Israel Jacobson in 1925 and for 15 years they had been worshiping in relative anonymity.[10] That would all change with the arrival of Rebbe Schneerson. But not immediately.

The dramatic break with his homeland and all the traditions of Eastern European Jewry was not an easy decision to make, and naturally it weighed heavily on Schneerson. In one sense, moving to the New World would keep the Lubavitcher heritage alive, but by the same token, he would be leaving an entire Lubavitcher community without direction. The survival of the Lubavitch sect took precedence; it always had been a group of resilience and survivors. The Lubavitchers were Jews who practiced Chabad Hasidim, and Joseph Schneerson was the sixth rebbe of the sect, which dates its history back to medieval times in Eastern Europe. It is a history of trials, tribulations, and mysticism that began in the woods of Poland and was transported to other parts of Europe, including Russia and later the world.

Mystical Beginnings

The journey of Lubavitcher Hasidim begins with Shneur Zalman, the first Lubavitcher rebbe and the founder of the Lubavitcher dynastic "court."[11] In Hasidim the term *court* is used to describe or define a group of like-minded Hasidic Jews who adhere to a certain and specific set of practices, beliefs, and traditions. Hasidism is a branch of the Jewish religion, which itself has many different groups of believers. Judaism is currently divided into three basic groups: Orthodox, Conservative, and Liberal. These categories define the degree of adherence to ancient traditions and customs within a group. For example, the Orthodox Jews are devoted to the ancient traditions; the conservatives do not put as much emphasis on those customs, and the liberal group, even less. Naturally there are more complex issues involved in the divisions between the groups concerning interpretations of the Talmud and other scriptures, but this suffices as a perfunctory overview.[12]

Although it is not completely agreed on, Hasidic Jews are largely grouped under the Orthodox category. Many Hasidic people would probably tell you that Hasidism actually is more orthodox than the Orthodox group; that is, they are more conservative and cling to even the most minute traditions, customs, and teachings of ancient Judaism. That may be true, but it may be more accurate to state that Hasidic Jews are more in tune to the mystical nature of Judaism and of nature and, as a result, find themselves living outside mainstream Judaism and outside the Orthodox group, as well.[13] In her personal journey into the Hasidic World entitled *Holy Days*, Lis Harris explains where Hasidism originates and what it means:

> The Hebrew word Hasid means, literally, pious one, and has always denoted a kind of spiritual rigorousness. The word is mentioned in the book of Psalms and in the Apocrophyl books of Maccabees, One and Two. In the second century, B.C., in Palestine, a group called the Hasideans joined in the revolt of Judas Maccabaeus against the Hellenized Syrian Antiochus Epiphanes, who attempted to Hellenize the Jews. These Hasideans, although known for their purity and saintliness, were not considered to be in any way different from their fellow Jews (as, later the Hasidim were); but they were admired by their co-religionists for their intense piety and stubborn faithfulness to their religion in the face of persecution.[14]

The history of Hasidim, as Harris and numerous other historians note, is complex due to the various dynastic courts that branched off from the original Hasideans. Many of these groups either broke away from the original tree or evolved through the years. But the roots of the tree lie in the medieval period around the time of the Crusades. It begins with the Kabbalistic teachings of the Hasideans, who believed and reveled in the mystical nature of the world and their environs. The origins of this group were traced by the eminent Jewish historian Simon Dubnow who, in his work *The History of the Jews in Poland and Russia*, explains that the medieval Hasidean movement took place as a result of the anti-Semitic attacks of the crusaders in and around the year 1175.[15] These attacks forced the Jews of Europe into hiding and to adopt methods of survival. As a result, many of these kabbalists moved away from the cultural centers, becoming ascetics, living and worshiping on the fringe. As Harris explains, this form of Hasidim is different than the one that appeared in the 1700s: "Unlike his eighteenth century namesake, the medieval Hasid was an ascetic, a man who was warned against even the innocent pleasures of keeping birds or spending time with children."[16]

These medieval Hasideans left a written legacy of their beliefs and teachings called the *Book of Pious*. Along with the *Book of Brilliance*, it would serve as a basic guide to the mystical, kabbalistic worship that would define Hasidism of the later period. That Hasidic period began in 1642 amid turbulence and controversy for Eastern Europe's Jews.[17]

Poland had seen an enormous increase in the Jewish population during the later stages of the medieval period. It is considered to be the place where the Yiddish language developed, arriving on the tongues of Jewish immigrants from Germany, speaking a dialect known as "middle German" and incorporating Hebraic and Slavic.[18] It was a place where Jews were tolerated, and as a result, the community flourished. In 1551 the Jews were granted autonomy within the kingdom by Sigismond II, and they began to develop their own "state within a state."[19]

But this flourishing period was short lived, the result of external forces at work in the Polish kingdom. The oppression of the Polish nobility stirred a rebellion among the peasantry of Eastern Europe, the Ukraine, and the White mountains. The ensuing violence once again relegated the Jews of the area to the sad reality of second-class citizenship. When the Ukrainian peasants rioted, the Jews found themselves targets of resentment. Once again the Jews were forced with the dilemma of emigration or persecution. In *The World of Hasidism*, Harry Rabinowicz describes this "catastrophe" for the Polish Jews:

> The climax came under the leadership of a peasant called Bogdan Zinov Chmielnicki (1593–1657), who had been wronged by an arrogant Polish overlord. Encouraged by their priests, an unholy alliance of Tartars, Cossacks and peasants wreaked venomous vengeance, "with fire and sword," on the defenseless Jews, whom they regarded as the agents and allies of their oppressors. Hell was unleashed and a reign of terror began for the "heretical Pole and unbelieving Jew." In the battle of Kniazhey Biarak on May 6, 1648, the Polish Army was annihilated. With the death of the Polish King, Wladyslaw, the way was open for Chmielnicki to march unopposed through the Ukraine, White Russia, Lithuania and Poland.[20]

What had developed was a culture of enduring oppression, a community that became highly insular for protection and survival. The insular nature of the community created a need for religious leaders who could transcend the esoteric practices of Judaism and move in a direction of kaballistic mysticism. From this point Hasidim would become a religious sect revolving around a charismatic, monolithic leader, whereas in the past the sect had been doctrine driven. Hasidim would become a dynastic culture.

The first and most enduring of these charismatic leaders would be Rabbi Israel Baal Shem Tov, known as the Besht, whom many consider to be the founder of modern-day Hasidism. Others point to Shem Tov as the man who popularized the movement and brought it to the masses. What historians agree on is the notion that the Hasidism of the Besht was a necessary ingredient for the Jews of Poland during a time of suffering at the hands of oppressive Christian governance.

The death of the Besht had much the same effect on Hasidism as the death of Mohammed on Islam: Many sects sprang up with various leaders and differing interpretations of Hasidic law. Finally, a disciple named Schneur Zalman of Liady emerged with a branch of Hasidism called Chabad, which would later be called Lubavitch Hasidim, named for the town that would later become its home.

Zalman had been born in Russia in 1745 and studied there as a rabbinical student. His ideas on Chabad are explained by Edward Hoffman in *Despite All Odds*:

> Rabbi Schneur Zalman viewed the process (of unifying the body with its original source) of spiritual growth as life-long, requiring tireless self-discipline and the appropriate use of both intellect and emotion. The system was called Chabad, an acronymic abbreviation of the Hebrew terms of the higher faculties of wisdom (chochmah), understanding (binah), and knowledge (daath). For this reason, his followers have, for two centuries, been known as Chabad Hasidim as well as Lubavitchers, after the town that eventually became their communal base.[21]

Zalman handed the dynastic reins of Lubavitch to his son, Dov Baer, who is credited with moving the sect to Lubavitch, Russia. From this point on, the rebbe would be a direct descendant, not necessarily by blood, but also through marriage, of Schneur Zalman. Chabad Lubavitch had become a dynastic court.

The storm clouds of World War I and the Bolsheviks effectively forced the movement of the Lubavitchers to Poland and ultimately the United States, where in 1925 a small community of Lubavitchers emerged in New York City. By 1940 Joseph Schneerson, the Lubavitch rebbe would arrive in America and join this small but burgeoning community in Crown Heights, Brooklyn.

CHAPTER

4 A CHANGING COMMUNITY

"WHEN WE ORGANIZE OUR PATROL, WHEN MEN MEET MEN, WE WILL SEE THEN WHAT THE PEOPLE IN THE LONG BLACK COATS WILL DO."
– REVEREND HERBERT DAUGHTRY, JUNE 23, 1978[1]

Crown Heights in 1964 was a neighborhood undergoing profound changes. The Dodgers had left the neighborhood nine years previous, breaking the hearts of not only the "Bleacher Bums," their infamous loyal fans, but the community also. Where home plate had stood for close to a century, at the corner of Sullivan Street and Bedford Avenue, there was nothing. No excitement, no fans, and no business. Soon a housing development would rise up with the name Ebbets Field, but the neighborhood would never be the same. The roar of the crowd for Jackie Robinson and Duke Snider would be replaced by screams of a different kind: fear and misery.

Perhaps Walter O'Malley had read the handwriting on the wall, or he was ahead of the trend, but either way, the departure of the Dodgers coincided with the demise of the neighborhood.[2] The area of Crown Heights surrounding Ebbets Field, Franklin Avenue to Rogers Avenue, Eastern Parkway to Empire Boulevard, had been known in police jargon as a "clubhouse," which meant that it was a nice place for a cop to work and walk the beat. By the mid 1960s that was no longer the case. In fact, it was just the opposite. The area had fallen so quickly that it had become unsafe even for the cops. And the slide would continue on into the 1990s.

A few blocks away, near Kingston Avenue and Eastern Parkway, the new rebbe of the Lubavitch Hasidim, Menachem Mendel Schneerson, was contemplating what his congregation should do. Most of the Whites had fled the area, which included Jews,

Irish, Italian, and another sect of Hasidim called the Bobovers. Crime was one of the issues, but it wasn't the only one. There were overtones of racial prejudice, of fear within the community. When the black faces started appearing on the block, many of the neighbors simply picked up and left. Some of this White Flight was the product of a tactic called blockbusting, a scheme by real estate developers where houses are purchased with the hidden intention of sale to a black family in order to get a foothold in the neighborhood, paving the way for future purchases by Blacks at greatly reduced property values. And some of it was simply ignorance and old-fashioned prejudice.[3] In *Jews of Brooklyn*, Mark Naison describes an idyllic, well-adjusted neighborhood, a description that would contrast starkly with the exodus of Whites in the mid 60s:

> Racial boundaries in Crown Heights, at least on the surface were far less oblivious. In the 1950's there were only a sprinkling of black families in the fifteen blocks between Eastern Parkway and Kings County Hospital, and most of them seemed working class. None of my neighbors seemed to fear the black people in our midst or worry about the children's behavior. The poor and troubled families in the neighborhood, the ones everybody felt sorry for, were all white.[4]

But Schneerson and his people were no longer living in 1950 New York City, although that was the year that Schneerson succeeded his father-in-law, Joseph Schneerson, as the Lubavitcher's seventh rebbe.[5] The reality of 1964 was a Crown Heights with increasing crime, and the Lubavitchers were feeling this reality. The question was whether they should follow the lead of the Bobovers and relocate to a safer, more congenial atmosphere. When Schneerson arrived at his decision, it was a momentous and historical occasion for Crown Heights as Jerome Mintz described it: "The Rebbe came out with the call not to move at a farbrengen. 'Here we stop.' This was the Rebbe's call and obviously Hasidim listened to him and didn't move."[6]

As a result of the rebbe's decision to stay in Crown Heights, an enterprising Hasidic man named Samuel Shrage formed a local patrol called the Maccabees, after the Biblical group.[7] Composed of local Lubavitchers, this group began patrolling the streets of Crown Heights, particularly around 770 Eastern Parkway and its environs, from midnight until dawn every night. But what started as an apparently altruistic endeavor quickly turned into a controversial and divisive issue in the community. Soon the black community was accusing the Maccabees of what would much later be called racial profiling. At the time, the local Blacks simply stated that the Lubavitchers were going out of their way to intimidate any Blacks they came across in the neighborhood.[8] This would become a long-standing point of controversy, one of the first harbingers of trouble.

In a *Village Voice* article, Joe Conason attributes the origin of the controversy to the Macabbees and to Rabbi Samuel Shrage. Shrage was a Brazilian immigrant. After joining the Lubavitchers he was one of the organizers of the Macabbees. This was a patrol of Hasidic Lubavitcher men who roamed the streets of Crown Heights. Many in the neighborhood viewed them as nothing more than vigilantes. There were numerous confrontations in the neighborhood over the years because the Macabbees could be described as cavalier in their attitude toward stopping people they viewed as outsiders in their neighborhood. Yet these "outsiders" were almost always neighborhood black men and teens.

> Shrage as the leader of the Maccabees came into direct confrontation with Sonny Carson, one of the black national activists. "At one point a confrontation between Shrage and Carson nearly came to blows. But he was the type of person whom Carson later respected, because Shrage was blunt, honest and unafraid."
>
> Conason also pointed out that Shrage was never held highly in Brooklyn machine politics. When Beame took office in 1973 Shrage was fired from his job in city government.[9]

When the rebbe decided to stay in Crown Heights, he set in motion what would become another controversial endeavor in the community. With the neighborhood changing demographically and as crime started to rise, many other Jewish congregations opted to leave the neighborhood for safer, if not more familiar surroundings. These groups left behind their significant religious edifices, some of which the Lubavitchers bought with the intent to develop. Once the call was to remain in Crown Heights, the plan was to expand the community and to somehow control it. The next step was to begin buying residential housing. Here, another enterprising Lubavitcher stepped in and availed himself of the federal housing grants in the neighborhood. His name was Mendel Shemtov, who would become a major actor in the entire Crown Heights drama as it unfolded over the years. But his earliest endeavors were in the area of housing:

> As a testimony to their determination to remain in Crown Heights the Lubavitcher Hasidim undertook an expensive renovation of their besmedresh [place of worship].
>
> Now that other Jewish Groups had abandoned the neighborhood, the Jewish Council fell into Lubavitcher control, and they used it to organize their economic and social campaign to maintain the stability of the neighborhood.

> One of the Hasidim who emerged as a secular leader of the Lubavitcher community was Mendel Shemtov, an energetic and intelligent businessman who had a gift for bringing people together. (Came from the Soviet Union and became a manufacturer in America)
>
> ... Shemtov became a strong figure in the Jewish Community Council and they began to buy properties at discounted rates.[10]

What ended up happening was a form of "blockbusting" but in reverse. In *The Crown Heights Neighborhood Profile*, Toby Sanchez dissected the Lubavitcher housing strategy and its effect on the neighborhood as a whole. First Sanchez explained the old pattern and then the change in strategy implemented by the Lubavitchers:

> The one group of Whites which did not run away was the Lubavitcher Hasidim, who came to Crown Heights in 1940. They decided that they would stay permanently in Crown Heights and rejected the "in-out pattern" of many other Jewish Neighborhoods.
>
> Not for Crown Heights the familiar cycle of settlement, mass influx, the building and flourishing of Jewish institutions only to be followed by desolation, decline, infusion of poorer elements, abandonment, panic and finally desolution. (Rabbi Yisroel Rosenfeld, Crown Heights Today, Crown Heights Jewish Community Council, no date but appears to be 1980.)[11]

The effort took on a life of its own, but simultaneously began to exert economic pressure in the community. One of the byproducts of this, whether intentional or not, was that the Blacks who had resided in the neighborhood before many of the new Lubavitchers had landed in America were now being pushed aside and losing their housing:

> The Crown Heights Community Corporation, a federally funded anti-poverty organization, operated from the late 60's to the late 70's providing youth, employment, housing and commercial revitalization programs. Most of its efforts were multi-racial and it was particularly effective on Utica Avenue before and after the blackout of 1977. Those who lead the Community Corporation now lead the Crown Heights Jewish Community Council.
>
> The strongest organization in Boards 8 or 9 is the Crown Heights Jewish Community Council, the secular arm of the Lubavitchers, which provides

services to all age groups, job seekers, small business and everyone else within its constituency. Chevra, its housing branch, has been the main housing developer in all of Crown Heights, renovating many buildings with low interest Participation loans, Article 8A Loans, Section B subsidies and whatever else was available. For years rumours have circulated that Chevra harasses black tenants out in order to do a renovation and afterwards rents to only a token few black families.[12]

This was something that did not begin immediately. As the 1960s grew more tumultuous, with Civil Rights unrest, increasing tension in the black ghetto, and higher crime rates, places like Crown Heights became less desirable neighborhoods in which to live. The buildings were dilapidated, the landlords were losing money, and one of the viable alternatives seemed to be either federally subsidized housing projects or arson for insurance money. The Lubavitchers took advantage of this market and began buying in earnest. As the 60s gave way to the 1970s, the endeavor picked up steam and also resentment from the black community.

CHAPTER 5

A CITY IN DECLINE: WAGNER, LINDSAY, BEAME, AND KOCH

When a city slides inexorably into the urban abyss of financial ruin, rising crime, and declining social services, government has broken its contract with the citizenry. Naturally the causes are as complicated as urban life itself. When the city sliding down that slope is the biggest city in the world, the epicenter of finance, culture, and media, the story becomes even bigger and the consequences more dire. When New York City finally hit bottom in early 1975, the crash could be heard around the world. And of course the finger-pointing and the blame game began in earnest.

But the road to financial ruin can be a winding road with many points along the way where the slide might have been stopped. Of course, when there is a crash, the driver of the car is considered to be at fault. In the case of New York City the road to ruin was long and winding, but there were many drivers who must share the blame, namely the line of mayors Robert Wagner, John Lindsay, and Abraham Beame. By the time Ed Koch took control of New York City in 1978 the damage had been done, and the recovery process was under way. Although it was Beame who ultimately was blamed for the collapse of the city, his culpability is only part of the story.

At the root of the problem seems to be a continuous history of financial mismanagement and a fatal lack of vision. There seemed to be a collective failure in New York City government to understand that there were major budgetary problems as early as 1963, and these problems only loomed larger in the years to come. In the case of such a monumental and complete collapse, it appears that the causes are part of an overall failure, an endemic and entrenched theory of government, and budgetary economics that not only did not work, but drove a city to financial collapse. The fact that it took more than 12 years to change course and save the city only exacerbated the problem. During the 12-year period in question there are a few common denominators. One of them is the Democratic Party, which had ruled New York City for most of the twentieth century, and the other is Abe Beame, who was the controller of New York City from 1964 until his election to mayor in 1974.

When a party controls almost every facet of city government for such an extended period, the praise for success and the blame for failure must reside with it. In the case of the New York City's financial collapse, it would seem that the Democratic Party bears the lion's share of the blame. Since the days of Tammany Hall, the Democrats essentially controlled New York City.

The year 1964 represented the twilight of Robert F. Wagner's 12-year reign as the mayor of New York City. It was a run that seemed in retrospect as benign as the decade in which it began.[1] But the issues of 1964, especially the Harlem riot, would offer glimpses of a future New York, a future with dark clouds on the horizon; labor troubles, racial struggles, and financial woes. It was a time of increased building in the city and not a lot of controversy. But by the end of his administration, New York City was starting to show some strain. More than just social, the problems were economic. Wagner had not given the store away to the unions, and as a result, they were becoming discontented. Crime was starting to increase in the poorer areas, and other economic problems were on the horizon. In his obituary in the *New York Times*, James Clarity referred to the Wagner years with a question: "Was It the Good Old Days or Crisis to Come?" In the article, Clarity describes the urban changes occurring during Wagner's three terms as mayor of the city, and traces the advent of John Lindsay as a candidate for that office who offered solutions for a "city in crisis."[2]

Lindsay's appearance on the political scene signified the first time in a long time that a non-Democratic candidate won the office of mayor. Although Lindsay ran as a Republican, history would show that he was anything but. In fact, Lindsay would wind up changing political affiliations for his ill-advised run at the Democratic nomination for president in 1972.

Winning the New York City mayoral election in 1965 with a slim majority of the vote by using a coalition of Liberals and Democrats who were disenchanted with machine politics, Lindsay represented a fresh face and a fresh approach to politics-as-usual in New York. Unfortunately, his administration was immediately beset with problems, including a transit strike on New Year's Day, the day of his inauguration. Although that strike would set the tone for the next years of labor negotiations, there were already myriad other problems inherited from Wagner's 12 years.

In the years following World War I, New York City experienced two profound socioeconomic changes: an increasingly larger influx of poor Blacks and Hispanics into a city that could not provide jobs nor could it afford to provide financial sustenance. And there was a major exodus of manufacturing and revenue-producing industry from the city. As a result, the city was losing a major tax base while the demand on social services increased. Wagner's administration must have recognized this dilemma, yet chose to continue the practice of borrowing against the future. When Lindsay took office he attempted to change this strategy, but ultimately succumbed to business as usual. His labor problems only exacerbated an already-difficult economic situation.

Another issue, not exclusive to New York City, was the exploding urban racial unrest and the controversy of the Civil Rights Movement. Robert Wagner had only a short time to deal with the fallout of the Harlem Riot of 1964. A harbinger of events to come, this riot announced the profound changes in the sociopolitical landscape of not only New York City, but the nation as well.

For John Lindsay, the Civil Rights Movement and issues concerning the poor and disadvantaged of New York City were of prime concern. But Lindsay had campaigned on the idea that he was not from the "old politics." He was not one of the city's "powerbrokers" and he truly believed in the Civil Rights issues that were troubling the nation at the time of his election and afterward. He believed in equality but was taking the reins of a city that was becoming increasingly divided ethnically and racially. In the epic *Beyond the Melting Pot*, Nathan Glazer and Daniel Patrick Moynihan attempt to explain and describe this racial-ethnic dynamic at work in New York City:

> Consider the politics of New York City. Major changes are now taking place in the city. The power of the regular Democratic Party—the "machine"—to name its candidates has been broken. [Wagner's election with the help of the Puerto Rican and Jewish middle-class voters was enough to overcome the opposition of Italian, Irish, and white Protestant middle-class and working upper-class voters.]
>
> For in New York City ethnicity and class and religion are inevitably tied to each other. The votes of the poor and the well-to-do cannot be understood without looking into the question of who the poor and well-to-do are, without examining their ethnic background.[3]

Their political and socioeconomic analysis and assessment of New York City was prescient and hauntingly predictive. Glazer and Moynihan had conducted extensive research and concluded: "Ethnicity and race dominate the city, more than ever seemed possible in 1963. That was, after all, before the first summer riots."[4] These conclusions did not bode well for the residents of New York City, especially this point in relation to race:

> But New York City, *Beyond the Melting Pot* argued, while it was America, was also different from America. It accentuated and heightened one distinctive goal of American society: its openness to new groups and its even handed distribution of opportunity. Here, the larger American experience of the Negro, based on slavery and repression in the South, would be overcome as the Negroes joined the rest of society, in conflict and accommodation, as an ethnic group.
>
> It didn't happen.[5]

That it didn't happen was not necessarily John Lindsay's fault. But Lindsay does figure prominently in the unraveling of New York City's financial situation. He had inherited a city with many economic and financial problems on the horizon, and his political legacy is that he did very little to confront those problems. By the election of 1974 it was apparent to everyone that the winner was inheriting a huge problem. The winner of that election could not have been surprised at the situation he found on assuming office, because he had been the New York City controller for the previous 12 years.

"If you don't know the buck, you don't know the job,"[6] were the words Abe Beame used to campaign for the mayor's job in 1974. These words got him elected, and then came the financial problems. But Beame knew about them as early as 1965 when he publicly advised Mayor Robert Wagner, "This is a time for a hard look at distasteful facts. It is also a time for a change in top-level fiscal policy."[7]

Wagner and Beame had fallen out politically that year and the feud erupted in the papers with that quote. Wagner had already criticized Beame for his intense affiliation with the Democratic machine politics that Wagner had been so successful in defeating in the previous mayoral election. Citing Beame's "bossism," Wagner backed Paul Screvane in the Democratic primary. But push had come to shove, and Beame prevailed. Now Wagner was faced with crossing parties and backing Lindsay or mending fences with Beame. Announcing that Beame had demonstrated a move toward democracy in the Democratic Party, Wagner supported Beame in the election.[8] There is little question as to whether Beame had ever really eschewed the machine.

If Lindsay was anathema to party machine politics, Abe Beame was its poster boy. His ascension to City Hall in 1974 was a celebration of the return of the Democratic Club and the beginning of the end financially for the city. In *City for Sale*, Jack Newfield and Wayne Barrett recalled Beame's unabashed defense of machine politics:

> In May 1974, four months into his term as mayor, Beame had been the guest of honor at [Meade] Esposito's annual Brooklyn county dinner and given a ringing defense of clubhouse politics:
>
> "We are sometimes accused of running a strong county organization. Critics call it a machine. But Brooklyn has demonstrated that effective party organization need not be synonymous with smoke-filled rooms. Rather, it is a vital force in the American party system ... I have been a member of the Brooklyn Democratic organization for the last forty years. I have always been proud of my membership and my pride has increased. No one, no one need apologize for being part of this kind of party organization."[9]

In *A Political Life: The Education of John V. Lindsay*, Nat Hentoff succinctly summarized Lindsay's dire straits:

> Lindsay would rule an almost bankrupt metropolis facing almost incurable problems, yet New York was still full of money and of people with great vitality and creative talent.[10]

Like a bad relay team, Wagner handed the stick to Lindsay, having blown a good lead. Lindsay handed the stick to Beame with the team in last place and the race over. Beame must have known it was coming and couldn't have been surprised at the situation, having been part of the inner workings of City Hall, especially the financial strategies. By 1975 those problems materialized on the front page of the *New York Daily News* with the headline: "FORD TO CITY: DROP DEAD."[11]

While this headline told city residents that they would not be bailed out by a Republican president named Gerald Ford and the federal government he controlled, it didn't tell them how the mess had begun and why it had gotten out of control. What city residents did know was that in 1975 New York City's finances were now controlled by a group of financiers and bankers called the Municipal Assistance Corporation led by Felix Rohatyn and that, in an unprecedented move, cops and firemen had been laid off the city's payroll in 1974 as Mayor Beame attempted to stave off financial and political ruin.[12] In *Abuse of Power*, Wayne Barrett and Jack Newfield explain the situation in which Abe Beame found himself and his inability to avoid it:

> Beame could not do what had to be done because he believed in the system, the same system that had created both him and the crisis. Like Mrs. Perlman, Beame was conditioned to say no first, and then wait, and delay, and hope the problems would solve themselves or go away. But New York's new problems, building up for fifteen years, could not be solved by the automatic no.[13]

As one door was closing, another was opening. The demise of Abe Beame meant the rise of another Democrat, Ed Koch, who would go on to three consecutive terms as mayor, following in the illustrious and auspicious footsteps of Gotham's only other three-term mayors, Bob Wagner and Fiorello LaGuardia. Koch was something of a Populist with a knack for well-timed conversions to popular thinking or perhaps ideas that he thought would net votes. Beginning as a liberal political activist in Greenwich Village, Koch took on the political machine of Carmine DeSapio and could brag of early success. Henceforth, Koch was clearly anti-machine, a candidate outside the political clubhouse and making sure that everyone knew it. He won the election of 1978, although an underdog, but not without clubhouse assistance.[14] As Jack Newfield and Wayne Barrett point out in *City for Sale*, without the help of Meade Esposito and the Brooklyn Democratic Club, Koch could have been just another also-ran.

CHAPTER 6 WELCOME BACK TO THE CLUBHOUSE

Carmine DeSapio and Tammany Hall. Meade Esposito and the Brooklyn Democratic Club. Stanley Steingut and the Madison Democratic Club of Crown Heights. They are or were once the ubiquitous "political machine;" "the clubhouse." From its earliest days, New York City has been the home of clubhouse politics. In 1789 a social club, The Society of St. Tammany, ironically limited in early membership to native-born Americans, was the first vestige of the political machine that would dominate New York City politics for nearly two centuries. Quickly, politicians discovered the advantages of a ready-made voting bloc, among them Aaron Burr who used the club to further his progress within the Democratic Party.[1] By the middle of the nineteenth century, Tammany Hall was controlled by the Irish for the Irish. It provided jobs in exchange for votes and money for the bosses. By the latter half of the twentieth century, Tammany Hall was controlled by an Italian-American, Carmine DeSapio, a strange mixture of progressive New Deal ideals and backroom, old-style politics. DeSapio ruled Tammany Hall and New York City until 1958, when he split with Robert Wagner. Around the same time, Ed Koch, who was working within the Village Independent Democratic Club (V.I.D.), was able to unseat a weakened DeSapio in 1963, which would be, in some respects, a watershed for the Democratic Party in New York City.[2]

While Koch was working his way up the ladder in the V.I.D., Abe Beame had already been a stalwart in Stanley Steingut's Madison Democratic Club of Crown Heights. And it is with Abe Beame's administration that the saga of Crown Heights took a controversial turn.

The Creation of Community Board #9

Tensions had been rising in Crown Heights since the creation of the Maccabees, the Lubavitcher community patrol, in 1964, and the situation continued to deteriorate throughout the 1960s. The crime rate continued to rise, as did the influx of Hasidim into the neighborhood. This influx created its own tension as Hasidics were now vying for subsidized housing with the Blacks and Hispanics who had been residing there all along. By the time Abe Beame took office, it was apparent that there was a problem in Community Board #8, which covered Crown Heights and additional territory all the way north to Atlantic Avenue. This situation was not acceptable to the Lubavitchers who lobbied for a redistricting.

Initially the idea was not well received, but with some intensive and well-placed lobbying, Beame reconsidered and ultimately influenced enough members of the Board of Estimate to follow his lead, which resulted in the creation of a new Community Board #9 for Crown Heights. This development had met with staunch opposition from the black political community, particularly from Reverend Herbert Daughtry, who related the developments in his book, *No Monopoly on Suffering*:

> Under pressure from Councilmen Bobby Steingut and Ted Silverman, as well as from the Hasidim, Mayor Abraham Beame, after initially endorsing the Charter Commission's plans, reversed his position and changed the plan in 1976. He drew up his own plan, moving Planning Board No. 9's northern boundary from Atlantic Avenue to Eastern Parkway, and extending its southern boundary to Clarkson Avenue, thus enhancing the Hasidim's power base while diminishing the Black community's power base in Crows Heights.
>
> The Black Community Council of Crown Heights, led by Vernal Cave, tried to resist this encroachment on Black interests. On December 22, 1976, I, along with other community leaders, sat up half the night with Mayor Beame at Gracie Mansion, trying to dissuade him from using his influence to change the planning board lines.

Daughty's frustration is apparent as he describes the herculean efforts made by the various leaders of the black community and other political supporters, especially Percy Sutton, who was motivated by this event to throw his hat into the mayoral ring.

> Blacks, I knew, viewed the vote as yet another power struggle between Blacks and some Jews; and that Jews had won again. Significantly, no charges of anti-Semitism surfaced during this time.

Daughtry understood the political dynamic and who really had the power in New York City:

> I criticized the Hasidim for their misuse of power, and I also criticized our Black leaders for not organizing our people to exercise power for our own interests:
>
> Let us suppose that the Hasidic Jews had tried to ingratiate themselves or shall I say, tried to Uncle Goldstein their way to power. Do you think anything would have been gained? Probably here and there somebody would have felt sorry for them and given them a few jobs and some poverty bucks, but nothing really substantial.
>
> However, by organizing themselves first, then making demands, they made success depend upon their own strength. So, when those Rabbis actually went somewhere to negotiate for their people, they had several thousand outside.
>
> When Black preachers try to negotiate, we go by ourselves, then argue about who's going to be the spokesman, who will get the chance to make a television statement.
>
> So we don't get anything or we get a little if the "Power person" is in a good mood or if he can give us something without hurting himself for going against his own ethnic group.
>
> The group of ministers who went to see Mayor Abe Beame was not about to move him from his position. All we were able to get from him was that we were going to cause him another sleepless night. In other words, we had a just cause, we pleaded with reason and righteousness. We had all the right on our side, we had everything going for us, but power. The Mayor knew as well as I knew that most of us don't have enough influence over people to get ten people anywhere except to a free chicken dinner.
>
> I've got to say it bothers me. Until we can produce people like those in the Hasidim, we will always be begging, fighting each other over who gets to be spokesman, fighting each other over who gets next to the Mayor, or who's suppose[d] to represent power.[3]

Perhaps this was the issue that pushed Crown Heights closer to conflict. In Daughtry's lengthy narrative of events leading up to creation of the new district, he mentions Bobby Steingut as a player in the political drama. Bobby Steingut was the son of Stanley Steingut, the boss of the Brooklyn Machine, his own Madison Democratic Club of Crown Heights, and one of the most powerful men in New York politics. Stanley had inherited the reins from his father, Irwin, who himself had been the majority leader of the New York State Assembly years before his son would attain that office. Both father and son represented Crown Heights in the Assembly.[4] Stanley's son Bobby took up the yoke, ran the Madison Democratic Club, and eventually served as both a city councilman and a New York State legislator. As for the matter of the Community Board creation, it was no surprise to any political analysts or, for that matter, anyone who was paying attention, that Abe Beame, a longtime worker in the Madison Democratic Club, would follow the rule of a man named Steingut. Far from a surprise, it was a given, a political no-brainer.[5] This was best illustrated in a *New York Times* article written at the time of Beame's inauguration. The article traced Beame's political lineage from Irving Steingut through his son Stanley, considered to be the boss of the Brooklyn machine. Stanley was poised to assume the Speaker of the State Assembly's office, which had been held at one time by his father. With Beame as the mayor and two other Brooklyn politicos ensconced in public office, the Madison Democratic Club was flexing its' political muscles.

Grace Lichtenstein detailed the extent of their clout:

> "He's One of Us"
>
> On paper, in fact, the Madison Club—still run by Stanley Steingut—must rank as the most powerful political club in the state and furthermore, Brooklyn, the most populous county in the state, will count all of the Madison Alumni plus Governor-elect Hugh Carey as its favorite sons.[6]

It is not hard to understand why Abe Beame changed his mind on the redistricting plan for the Crown Heights neighborhood. The Steinguts still held enormous sway with Beame, and there was a contingent within Crown Heights who held enormous sway with the Steinguts. That contingent was the Lubavitcher Hasidic community. The power of the ballot box is one of the important elements of a political machine. In Crown Heights as in Williamsburg and Borough Park, Brooklyn, the Hasidic community had continuously demonstrated its ability to deliver votes. This ability was outlined by Judith DeSena in *People Power*: "In analyzing voter turnout in Greenpoint-Williamsburg, one finds the communities of color have the lowest rate, followed by white residents. The Hasidim vote at the highest rate. They vote as a block [sic] for the candidate sanctioned by the Rebbe, and go to the polls in response to the Rebbe's suggestion."[7]

As a voting bloc, the Lubavitcher Hasidim were rumored to have control of the politics in Crown Heights. For the black residents, the day-to-day political and governmental activities did not dispel this rumor. Reverend Herbert Daughtry not only recognized this situation but commented on it publicly. It was about this time (1977) that unhappiness in the black community became more pervasive and apparent. This was a momentous decision, not so much for the effect it had on the community, because it didn't really change the balance of power in terms of demographic proportions. Blacks still retained a solid majority of voters, even as the boundaries of the new district seemed gerrymandered to cater to the Hasidic minority. No, this was a momentous decision because it made evident to everyone involved that the Hasidic group seemed to control the political clubhouse and, therefore, controlled the community. Sometimes perception is reality whether or not it is real.

What followed was a decade of acrimony and confrontation that continued throughout the entire administration of Ed Koch, who, although he was not considered a clubhouse politician, was somewhat indebted to Meade Esposito for some well-timed political support during his first campaign. It has been asserted by Newfield and Barrett that Ed Koch was more than happy to let the political clubhouse bosses rule their individual fiefdoms without much outside interference. In *City for Sale*, the authors contend that many of the scandals that plagued his later years were the result of what might be considered tacit approval or a strategy of plausible deniability.[8] Koch did not want to appear beholden to the political machine, but *City for Sale* maintains that indeed he was. Quoting Brooklyn party boss Meade Esposito, who inherited the job from his business partner, Stanley Steingut, Newfield and Barrett make it clear just how things worked politically in Brooklyn:

> I get whatever I fuckin' want from [him]. I told him not to dump our captains, and he said no problem. He promised me access and that he would be a good mayor. He kept his word on both scores. He promised me he would promote Tony [Ameruso] and he did. He told that bullshit screening committee to fuck off when they tried to say Tony wasn't qualified. I admire that kind of balls. I told Koch that Tony is my guy and he showed respect for my judgement [sic].[9]

This discourse followed a meeting in which Koch had asked for Esposito's support in the 1977 mayoral election, support that was instrumental in his victory over Mario Cuomo. *City for Sale* underscores how difficult a move it was for Koch in seeking this support, which came with a heavy price tag:

> Yet for Koch, turning to the Brooklyn Boss for support meant allying himself to a man he had long disdained, a man he had described as a "gangster" to his friends. Esposito was the avatar of the machine politics that Koch

> had been fighting for the past fifteen years, the personification of the system of patronage and bossism that the young Koch and V.I.D. had vowed to eradicate. ... Jack Newfield had published a lengthy exposé of Esposito in the Village Voice called "Meade, the Mob and the Machine." Koch called Newfield to congratulate him and urged him to follow up on the investigation. ... He was a neon sign that said MACHINE BOSS.[10]

That there was a criminal element involved is not particularly relevant to the Crown Heights issue. What mattered in Crown Heights and in other neighborhoods in Brooklyn was where the money was going and to whom. Who was getting the jobs, who was afforded the housing, and who was availing themselves of the patronage. To the Blacks in Crown Heights it seemed much of this was going to the newcomers in the neighborhood: the Lubavitchers.

It was also during the Koch administration that racial tensions became exacerbated, not only in Crown Heights but also in New York City. Many political observers and activists attribute some of this to Ed Koch's propensity for polarizing public dialogue. Koch saw himself as a tell-it-like-it-is political persona, but to many people of color in the city his public pronouncements were divisive and hurtful. Others viewed it as ethnic politics at work, where a candidate or a public official has gauged where his loyalties and his power base lay and then caters almost exclusively to that group. The other groups often are left outside the tent. During the Koch administration this was a commonly voiced complaint, especially among black activists like Herbert Daughtry, who felt and later stated that Koch was a divisive demagogue:

> The previous twelve years of the Koch Administration, characterized by pettiness, meanness, belligerence, and corruption, fanned the flame of racial antagonism, instigating conflict—it was an anti-black, anti-poor administration. Nobody, short of God, could right these wrongs in four years.[11]

Daughtry's words were indicative and representative of the collective black activist and political community. He certainly was not alone in his feelings, which were echoed by many others throughout the 1980s, especially in Crown Heights. It seems that during this period Crown Heights became the battleground on which the black political activists would fight their war against what they saw as the injustices for Blacks of New York City and America. Indeed, Crown Heights soon became the proving grounds for a movement that would protest the inequities of housing, racial inequality, and white oppression, manifested by police brutality. Soon the drums of protest would be beating as various independent protest groups would march the streets of that neighborhood, taking up the cause of the locals and bringing the complaints of the black community as a whole to those streets. Crown Heights would become the stage on which a great drama would play out, culminating in the riot in 1991.

CHAPTER 7 THE POLITICS OF CONFRONTATION

"YOU COULD SEE BLOWS AND PUNCHES AND FISTS AND HEAR PEOPLE GASPING AND THEN THE LEFT GROUP HIT AND THERE IT WAS: CONFRONTATION."
– SONNY CARSON[1]

Early in Ed Koch's first term as mayor, a disturbance erupted in Crown Heights that would have repercussions into the early 1990s. In Rev. Herbert Daughtry's tome, *No Monopoly on Suffering*, the activist points to a number of incidents that occurred in Crown Heights that inflamed the racial tensions and reinforced the perception among Blacks that racial prejudice was at work, both in the streets in dealing with the police and within the Koch administration. One of those incidents was the beating of Victor Rhodes, a local black youth who, it was alleged by Daughtry (and supported by a police report), "was beaten unconscious by thirty to fifty Hasidim." To Daughtry the most disturbing element came next:

> Two Hasidim were arrested.
>
> During the trial, the Hasidim pulled one of their trick plays. On those rare occasions, when one of their members must stand trial, they all show up, obviously in black, this making individual identification virtually impossible. So they walk away laughing and joking, demonstrating again their utter contempt for the people they have assaulted and for the law they have violated.[2]

In his book, Daughtry continued with another case of "police brutality," which in this case turned deadly. Joe Conason wrote an article in the July 3, 1978 edition of the *Village Voice* describing a confrontation with the police that stemmed from a traffic stop. A black man named Arthur Miller was killed as he and his brother fought with the cops. It became a much larger brawl as the cops attempted to arrest the brothers. Arthur Miller, considered by many to be a pillar of the community, wound up dead as the result of the altercation. Of course this incited some major neighborhood unrest in Crown Heights.

After providing a narrative, Conason follows with his own analysis, hoping for a solution but arriving at a dramatic and, as it turns out, prophetic message: "If not this hot night, perhaps another."[3]

Ironically, the one leader who Conason felt had the savvy was the founder of the Maccabees, Rabbi Samuel Shrage. Of course Conason also understood the problems the Maccabees brought with them in their crime-stopping efforts. Rev. Daughtry was another person well aware of the Maccabees' issues among the others in Crown Heights.

For Daughtry and the Blacks of Crown Heights this was highly representative of the problems confronting them in their own neighborhood. Daughtry continued with another in the litany of injustices:

> Significantly, the day before Victor Rhodes was beaten, Arthur Miller, a respected businessman who went to see about his brother, who was in an altercation with the police, ended up dead, killed by the police. But in July 1977, the Hasidim, trying to capture three innocent Black youths they believed had committed a crime, took over the 71st Precinct. There were no arrests, not one Hasid was injured. In Boro Park, the Orthodox Community destroyed the police precinct—literally destroyed it. Forty Police Officers were hurt. Ed Koch was pleading with them in Yiddish. There was no tough talk, no "get more police on the case" as he urged Mayor David Dinkins to do during the recent eruption in Crown Heights. Not one Hasid was hurt or convicted of a crime ... unbelievable."[4]

In this instance Daughtry alludes to the riot in the 66th Precinct in which another sect of Hasidim stormed the station house and injured a number of officers. For Blacks and others in New York City, this incident became the classic illustration of the double standard applied to Hasidim. In *Hasidic People*, Jerome Mintz recalled the incident:

The attack on the 66th Precinct took place on December 2nd, 1978 when two hundred Hasidic protestors (many of them may have actually been members of the JDL).

"The four officers on duty were surprised by the sudden appearance of two hundred protestors who entered the station house while another two thousand gathered outside.

According to a few witnesses some of these men were "out to make trouble." The sergeant at the desk reported that "It got filled wall to wall with people ... we were literally fighting for our existence." The sergeant called for assistance and 170 policemen from a number of precincts responded to "patrolmen in trouble."

The Hasidim maintain that the protest was orderly until the police reinforcements arrived. As one Hasid described: "They came swinging their clubs, and one guy had a smile on his face while he was hitting people." As the blows rained down, they tried to shield their heads and then reacted angrily. In the ensuing thirty minutes, 72 persons were reported injured, including 62 policemen, a count regarded with skepticism by the Hasidim present.[5]

This incident was just another reminder to the black community and others in New York that the Hasidim packed a political punch, and could be counted on in the clutch to respond with overwhelming numbers, whether it be in the voting booth or in the street for a demonstration. That was one of the points Daughtry alluded to in criticizing the mayoral flip-flop on the redistricting of Community Board #8 and the creation of Community Board #9. Soon the rank-and-file of the New York Police Department would be referring to the 66th Precinct as "Fort Surrender," and it was no surprise to many cops when the 66th Precinct Club showed up at an off-duty police department social function in a Hasidic school bus with a Hasidic driver. It had been rumored for a year that the rabbi in the "6-6," as the cops called the 66th Precinct, would regularly walk behind the desk in the precinct, an area that was off-limits even to most cops, never mind a civilian dressed in Hasidic attire. Although some of these stories were probably exaggerations, they reinforced the belief that the Hasidim not only wielded considerable political clout, they also controlled the police.

These same allegations were being hurled about in Crown Heights. One of the focal points of public ire was the 24-hour police car stationed in front of 770 Eastern Parkway. Daughtry constantly addressed this issue:

> Another bone of contention was/is the ambulance and the police car parked in front of the Lubavitcher headquarters and the home of the Grand Rebbe, respectively. The car in front of the Grand Rebbe's home was to protect him from the Satmar in Williamsburg, at least that is what we are told. We complained bitterly that this was preferential treatment. The car was removed for a while and then returned and we were told the funding for the ambulance came from private money, which was not totally true ... part of the money came from the public. Of course things remained the same.[6]

Another issue that wouldn't go away was the composition of the community board, which Daughtry also lambasted:

> There is a disproportionate Representation of Hasidim on Community Planning Board 9 which encompasses Crown Heights. Half of the members of the Board of Directors are appointed by Brooklyn Borough President Howard Golden. While the other half are appointed by the City Council members representing the area, with the approval of the Borough President. Of the approximately 200,000 community residents, between 10 and 20% are Hasidim, yet the Hasidim make up 25%, of the Board, and the Boards' Chairperson is Rabbi Jacob Goldstein.
>
> For years Dr. Vernal Cave, a long-time Resident of Crown Heights, complained about the situation. In a letter written to Mr. Fletcher M. Graves, New York State Director of Community Relations Service, United States Department of Justice on June 28, 1978, Dr. Cave wrote:
>
> "High officials of New York City including then Mayor Abraham D. Beame, violated the civil rights of the Black Citizens of Crown Heights when in forming districts for community boards in accordance with provisions of New York City Charter as revised in 1975 it violated two of the three provisions it was legally obliged to obey."[7]

This division of one community board into two, as discussed earlier, had major repercussions within the community, and it was obvious that the creation of another community board consolidated the white population into one zone and to some extent, split American Blacks from Caribbean Blacks with the dividing line being Eastern Parkway. Previously the entire area stretched from Atlantic Avenue on the north to Clarkson Avenue as the southern boundary. With the redistricting, certain demographic shifts became apparent. In *Crown Heights Neighborhood Profile*, Toby Sanchez discussed these changes and how they affected community perception:

Residents interviewed for this Crown Heights Neighborhood Profile expressed both admiration and resentment of the Hasidic success in obtaining political attention and public funds. It is widely believed that the Lubavitchers can be counted upon to vote as a block [sic] in every election, from city wide offices, to Area Policy Board, to Community School Board #17 (despite the fact that Hasidic children do not attend public schools), and thus manage to get far more attention than their numbers would warrant. "They have every right to flex their muscles, and I have no problem with their getting their fair share, but they get far more. I believe in 1 man, 1 vote; 1 man, 1 dollar."—The interviewee was kept confidential by the author.

Many in Crown Heights believe that their needs are ignored and that "the majority is treated like a minority." For example, it is a constant complaint that diligent, fair police protection is not available in this high crime area where the majority of the victims are black, not white. People often complain that the budget crisis cut police manpower for everyone but the Hasidim. Police guard the home of Rabbi Schneerson every day (24 hours, 3 shifts, 2 persons per shift) and other police are assigned near the synagogues during the Sabbath, but there is no regular police protection at a notorious drug and mugging spot like Franklin Avenue and Eastern Parkway. Only when community complains is a van stationed there a short time, but it is soon withdrawn.[8]

But the changes Sanchez and the residents talk about in the Crown Heights redistricting were not as convincingly an advantage for the Hasidim. What the redistricting actually did was to take the Hasidic community out of the higher-crime community and most likely afford them lower insurance rates and other benefits. During this time, many of the police precincts in New York City were redrawn to correspond to the community district that the precinct served. This process was called co-terminality. In many incidences it had the effect of consolidating the higher crime areas in one precinct while the adjoining precinct then enjoyed a lower crime rate. In the early to mid 1980s in Brooklyn, co-terminality significantly changed the crime ratings of certain precincts. For example, the 71st Precinct was redrawn to correspond to Community Board #9, thereby losing some high-crime areas to the 77th Precinct and also to the 67th Precinct. Previously all three precincts were high-crime houses. After co-terminality, the 71st emerged with far less crime and a more working-class demographic. And all the Lubavitchers resided in Community Board #9 and in the 71st.

The demographics of Crown Heights after the redistricting as per the United States Census are represented in the tables below:

Neighborhood Population	1970	1980	% Change
All Crown Heights	222,868	185,846	–17%
CB#8	121,821	88,954	–27%
CB#9	101,047	96,892	–4%

Note: Most of the decline was north of Eastern Parkway in Community Board #8.

Population Change in Crown Heights	
Population Change Between 1970 and 1980 in	
New York City (all boroughs)	–10.4%
Brooklyn	–14.3%
Crown Heights	–17%
Community Board #8	–27%
Community Board #9	–4%

Population decline was far greater in Crown Heights than in Brooklyn or the city as a whole, but only the northern half suffered serious decline.

Racial and Ethnic Background				
	Whites	**Blacks**	**Hispanics**	**Asians**
1960	71%	27%	2%	–
1970	27%	68%	5%	–
1980	7%	81%	9%	2%

Crown Heights was white in 1960 and black in 1970.

	WHITES	%	BLACKS	%	HISPANICS	%	ASIANS	%
CB#8	4,845	5.4%	75,087	84.4%	7,501	8.4%	2,122	1.7%
CB#9	9,086	9.4%	75,964	78.4%	9,257	9.5%	2,586	2.7%

The table above shows that the white population in CB#9 is twice as large as that in CB#8, while the other racial and ethnic groups are of approximately equal size in both boards.

The black population is very mixed ethnically, composed of persons born in the North and the South, plus a very large percentage of first and second generation people from Jamaica, Barbados, Trinidad-Tobago, St. Lucia, St. Kitts, Grenada, Guyana, and Haiti.

The Hispanic population is composed of people from P.R., Dominican Republic, Panama, Honduras, and other countries of Central and South America.[9]

The following tables illustrate the socioeconomic disparities that exist not only in Brooklyn, but in the Crown Heights community, as well. Crown Heights was indeed a unique and complex neighborhood in Brooklyn, economically, ethnically, and racially. The creation of the new community board further exacerbated those disparities.

CARIBBEAN POPULATION DOCUMENTED AND UNDOCUMENTED–1980		
	Documented	**Undocumented**
Brooklyn	329,900	258,000
Manhattan	152,100	132,000
Queens	65,700	57,000
Bronx	111,000	89,500
Staten Island	6,600	–
TOTALS	665,300	536,500

Crown Heights Median Income Compared with Brooklyn Families by Race and Ethnicity		
	Median Family Income	**% of White Family Income**
Brooklyn White Families	$18,862	100%
Brooklyn Black Families	$11,559	61%
Brooklyn Hispanic Families	$8,952	47%
All Brooklyn Families	$14,664	78%
CB #8 Families	$10,540	56%
CB #9 Families	$13,002	69%

Source: Municipal Research Institute, Brooklyn in Transition, 1985, p. 27; A Socioeconomic Profile, pp. 118, 122.

In *Crown Heights Community Profile*, Sanchez broke down the crime statistics:

"Crime in Crown Heights"

Crown Heights suffers from a reputation as a high crime area and, unfortunately, the statistics confirm it. The two precincts serving the area (the 77th which is co-terminus with Community Board # 8, and the 71st, which is co-terminus to #9) both rank high in reported felonies.

Reported Crimes–Number and Borough Ranking				
	77th Precinct		**71st Precinct**	
	1985	**1986**	**1985**	**1986**
Murder & Non Neg Homicide	38	41	18	30
Forcible Rape	109	75	93	86
Robbery	1,897	2,144	1,253	1,498
Burglary	2,594	2,537	2,458	2,309
Grand Larceny Auto	629	774	821	904
Total Felonies	8087	8857	7724	7903

Three-Year Comparisons of Total Felonies			
	1984	**1985**	**1986**
71st Precinct	7,739	7,424	7,903
Borough Ranking	N/A	8th	9th
77th Precinct	7,749	8,087	8,857
Borough Ranking	N/A	7th	5th

Sources: "New York City Police Department Crime Comparison Report, 1985"; *New York Times*, April 5, 1986 and March 24, 1987.

Sanchez' study shows the geographical size of all the precincts in Brooklyn, with the 77th and 71st being small. There is a question about the validity of the Community Board restructuring and the accompanying co-terminality that restructured the police precincts to mirror that of the Community Board. When the 71st was restructured in 1982, the precinct lost a large portion of a high-crime area in the east 90s near the northeast corner of the old precinct boundaries. As a result, the crime statistics in the 71st dropped significantly—the crime levels were picked up by the 67th Precinct.

But Sanchez also acknowledges the overriding perception in the community: "The 71st Precinct, covering Community Board # 9, is also considered indifferent to the black community, because there the key to success for a commanding officer is to maintain good relations with the Hasidim and then you'll be promoted to something higher."[10]

Toby Sanchez' *Crown Heights Community Profile* was published in 1990 before the Crown Heights riot and was prophetic in tone. The problems that Sanchez documented in the *Profile* were clearly at the heart of the conflagration in 1991. But it was not all that difficult to assess these problems in the early 1990s as they were being proclaimed from the protest stages and bullhorns that became ubiquitous to the area in the late 1980s. In Crown Heights these were certainly Days of Outrage.

CHAPTER 8

THE DAYS OF OUTRAGE

Outside of the 71st Precinct where the demonstrators made a stop, Black activist lawyer Colin Moore told the cops, "You are here to protect the Hasidic community against the Blacks. We came to this country 360 years ago as slaves, we built the plantations; we built the cities and we are going to stay and get the rewards. We will not tolerate people who have recently come from certain European countries—who have come here themselves as refugees (and) victims of discrimination to abuse us."[1]

Those words shouted by Colin Moore told a story of history and predicted the future for Crown Heights. There had already been some protests in the neighborhood, but there would be more. There would also be protests in adjoining neighborhoods. One in particular in the Flatbush section would have great significance, and another, featuring most of the players in the Crown Heights protests, would wind up in a near riot at the Brooklyn Bridge.

Those "players" in Crown Heights, some of whom were already well known in the community, and others were attracted to the area for many reasons. Crown Heights embodied many of the issues intrinsic to the Civil Rights Movement that gained so much momentum in the 1960s, only to experience a period of decline through the 1970s. Although that decade certainly experienced its moments, by and large New York City was a city in financial distress during that time. In those days the issues were crime and the fact that New York City and its government seemed powerless to control crime. Either that or the politicians were unwilling to make the hard decisions needed to combat crime. But by the mid 1980s these old issues had once again risen to the surface. Of course these issues had never gone away; they had always been bubbling below the surface. By 1986 in Crown Heights the pot was getting hotter and it was now being stirred by a diverse group of dedicated activists who recognized that these issues could now be addressed.

SONNY CARSON

Blue police barriers frame the intersection of Nostrand Avenue where it intersects Empire Boulevard. Cops in riot helmets stand idly by watching with a mixture of indifference and curiosity. It is a hot May afternoon and the streets are surprisingly quiet, except for a small group of protestors marching down Nostrand Avenue to that intersection. They are shouting various slogans, especially "No Justice, No Peace!" Near the front of the group but not completely in front is a large, middle-aged black man with a salt-and-pepper goatee. He is wearing a kouffe cap and white robes. He is apparently the de facto leader of the protest group and his name is Sonny Carson. The first "Day of Outrage" has begun, and Carson is one of the main reasons. His checkered résumé includes "Freedom Riding" in Alabama, but also an extensive prison stay in upstate New York. Perhaps in the traditions of Malcolm X, Carson represents the quintessential black activist, although there are also deviations from that model. *The Education of Sonny Carson*, an autobiography under the name Mwlina Abubdika, includes arrests for drugs and robbery in the 50s followed by a conversion to the protest movement. In Robert "Sonny" Carson's own words:

> So for my first nineteen years the schoolhouses were the prisons and the prisons were the prisons posing as schoolhouses and the many sides of genocide continued to perpetrate itself, in whatever form.[2]

Carson was born in the Bedford-Stuyvesant section of Brooklyn, an area that was beginning to emerge as the second largest black neighborhood in the country. It would eventually be referred to as the Black Ghetto, perhaps a misnomer but a common usage nonetheless.[3] Carson vividly describes his old neighborhood:

> You see I lived in a white ghetto on the edge of a larger, white, middle-class community; and right in the middle of this white ghetto was a black outpost. In the white ghetto were mostly poor Irish and Italians and some Jews, and outside, in the middle class area were richer Jews. Bedford Stuyvesant, it was and is called, very close to Crown Heights, which was 100 percent Jewish: 75 percent middle class, 15 percent upper-middle class, and 10 percent orthodox (lower class). And about ten blocks away, the blacks were slowly occupying building after building and eventually occupying both communities, encircling our outpost, and occupying two-thirds of Crown Heights today.[4]

After his stay in prison Carson drifted for a while until he heard the words of Malcolm X, whom he credited with setting him on the right path. And that path was the Civil Rights Movement of the early to mid 1960s. Carson recalls the Malcolm X days:

> The first week in February 1965 found me at a large auditorium in Harlem. Waiting to hear that phenomenal black man speak. His name was Malcolm X and to listen to him, as far as I was concerned, was the most electrifying experience I have ever indulged in. This Brother who was the official spokesman in the area for The Honorable Elijah Muhammad, leader of the movement called the Black Muslims, brought to light a lot of the secret yearnings that I had about life and determining it for myself.[5]

Carson fell into the movement quickly and makes it clear that he espoused Malcolm X's philosophy and ironically did not initially look favorably on the teachings of Dr. King:

> At that same time, there was another Brother named Martin Luther King, who was beginning to upset me because that philosophy he taught was spreading and it didn't seem to fit right with me. That "turn the other cheek" business and-shee-it. Malcolm, I thinks was saying it right: that if someone hit you on one side of your check, then you lay him in the grave. Somehow I leaned to his philosophy even though found out later on that Brother King made as great a contribution as Malcolm.[6]

By 1968, one of the famous riot years for America and New York City, Carson was firmly entrenched in the Congress of Racial Equality (CORE) and very involved in negotiations with the Lindsay administration over areas under siege in Brooklyn. It was another incident later in 1968 that cemented Carson's legitimacy within the protest community, and he looks back fondly on the experience. Ironically it was the Ocean Hill-Brownsville school strike that brought to light a disturbing shift in black activist philosophy and was an early indicator of a rift in the "Liberal Jewish-Black coalition". Warning signs had been on the horizon earlier in the decade, but the events of the school strike in Brooklyn illustrated that, far from partners in protest, Blacks and Jews were now on opposing sides of an issue. And even more disturbing, for the Jews at least, was the vitriolic rhetoric being hurled across the picket lines by black protestors at people who had considered themselves their life-long ally. In the middle of it all was John Lindsay, another liberal caught between a rock and a hard place, and once again falling victim to his own naiveté.

Ocean Hill-Brownsville

It was obvious to anyone in New York City who cared that the education system had been severely lacking for years. Of course, one of the key issues had been integration of schools and the lack of equality in educational opportunities for children in impoverished neighborhoods, mostly black and Puerto Rican kids. Many solutions had been proposed and one of them was adopted in the Ocean Hill-Brownsville school district in Brooklyn. The strategy called for the superintendent of the school district and the principal of the school to have more autonomy from the Board of Education. This was implemented in Brownsville, and the principal of the school began to make some changes, some of which were radical and unpopular.

The most unpopular and radical idea was the firing of 13 teachers by Rhody McCoy, the black administrator, who deemed them unacceptable for the district. All but one of the teachers was White and Jewish. Immediately the Teachers Union intervened on behalf of the teachers and after initial negotiations, a protracted citywide strike took place. The Teachers Union was predominantly Jewish and their leader, Albert Shanker, himself was a Jewish liberal who admitted to be a former socialist. Shanker and the union dug in, and things grew tense. For many of the Jews on the Board of Education, this was a rude awakening. Until this point, many of them had considered themselves kindred spirits, if not brothers-in-arms with many of the Blacks, especially when it came to Civil Rights and education issues. One of the most disturbing developments occurred when one of the new black teachers, a militant named Leslie Campbell, read a poem entitled *Anti-Semitism* to Albert Shanker:[7]

The incendiary and vitriolic anti-Semitism expressed in the poem served up a harsh slap in the face to every Jewish liberal in Brooklyn, especially the teachers, who had ever been involved in the Civil Rights Movement, even if only offering support from a safe distance. Using terms like "Jew-boy," threatening and inferring violence and murder, the poem illustrated the resentment and hatred for Jews that was apparently bubbling to the surface in a segment of the black community.

But the war of words and the picketing were taking a toll. Many political observers viewed this situation as the moment in time when the coalition fell apart. But the handwriting had been on the wall for many years, as Marc Dollinger commented in his article entitled "A Different Kind of Freedom Ride: Jews and the Struggle for Racial Equality":

> When militant blacks purged whites from their organizations, they symbolically rejected Jewish liberal values. Moreover their advocacy of group based affirmative action programs threatened the meritocratic foundations

> of Jewish liberal reform instilled fears that less worthy minority candidates would usurp positions better reserved for more qualified candidates. The rise of Black Power exploded the myth that Jews and blacks shared common histories or destinies. In the minds of the new civil rights activists, Jewish philanthropy translated into nothing more than Jewish paternalism.[8]

Later in the article, Dollinger recognizes that the split had been coming and was hastened by the philosophy and rhetoric of Black Nationalism:

> Jewish leaders worried about the rise of black militancy as early as 1960, four years before the Black Power movement gained national prominence.
>
> [W]ith a membership estimated at 60,000 and 150,000, Edelstein identified these new followers of Islam as a "potent source of anti-Semitism" and explained that since the movement by "its nature is pro-Arab, it tends to make it anti-Jewish, and some of its elements are outspokenly so."[9]

Of course Dollinger's article was written with the benefit of historical perspective, which is not to say that the sharp rhetoric of Elijah Muhammad, Malcolm X, and later Louis (X) Farrakhan was not disturbing to Jewish liberals (and Whites in general) who had seen themselves as part of the solution and not part of the problem.

There had also been other indicators prior to the Ocean Hill-Brownsville debacle. In *The Confrontation* written in 1970, Max Geltman remarks:

> One may deduce that, although Jewish boys and girls were in the vanguard of those "going to Mississippi," the Jew is now in the unpleasant and dangerous position of scapegoat for the American Negro. As before, there will be no one to protect him.
>
> We need not be surprised therefore at the remarks of CORE leader Clifford H. Brown, who at a public meeting in Mount Vernon, New York on February 3, 1966, blurted out that "Hitler made one mistake when he didn't kill enough of you Jews." James Farmer's mild rebuff to his then subordinate prompted Will Mallow of the American Jewish Congress to resign from CORE, stating in the *Congress BiWeekly* that "racism is racism."[10]

CORE was the organization in which Sonny Carson was active and is what brought him to the picket lines outside one of the Ocean Hill-Brownsville schools. He said, "Already standing there on the steps of the school was a beautiful sight to behold: about thirty of our Brothers and Sisters, some with helmets on and all dressed in some sort of fatigue or battle dress. My heart went out to them."[11]

The dispute had brought Sonny Carson and Albert Shanker into direct confrontation; two men who may have been political allies in the early 1960s were now diametrically and virulently opposed. The solution to the problem had been brokered by Mayor John Lindsay, who unintentionally or perhaps ignorantly had left the black community out of the negotiations. When the decision to open the school was implemented by the police, the black community was infuriated and blocked the entrance, leading to Carson's quote at the top of this chapter. What ensued was a minor riot and what resulted was further distrust between two former political allies, liberal Jews and Blacks. The Ocean Hill-Brownsville School strike was a harbinger of tense and controversial times in Brooklyn as the battleground eventually shifted to Crown Heights.

Ocean Hill-Brownsville was an event that defined Sonny Carson and his politics of confrontation, and also raised fears among Jewish and white New Yorkers as to the nature of Black Nationalism. It was a chapter in New York race relations that would have lasting repercussions in both communities. The Jewish community felt betrayed by the very people they felt allied with in many causes; the black community, which was left out of the negotiations among Lindsay, the Board of Education, and the United Federation of Teachers also felt betrayed. Of course the big losers in the whole mess were the children who missed so much school while this sociopolitical drama played out on the stage that is New York City.

"The New York 8"

As Sonny Carson and his group of protestors continued marching on the first "Day of Outrage," it became apparent that many of the rank-and-file cops manning the barricades knew some of the protestors by name. Yes, they knew the Rev. Herbert Daughtry by face because of his high-profile media battles with the mayor and others in NYC government, and they knew Al Sharpton because he had made a name for himself on the stage of Bensonhurst and Howard Beach when those communities went through their own race-related tragedies: the killing of black men because they were black and happened to be in their neighborhoods at the wrong time (if there was a right time?)!

But the cops seemed to know the names and faces of some of the other marchers, people who weren't famous, people who hadn't been seen on TV or heard on radio. Yet the cops knew them by name and remarked to each other about these people. One of them was Coltrane Chimurenga, one cop said he was a Ph.D. from Harvard. Another was named Roger Wareham, and someone said he was a lawyer from Columbia. One of the women was recognized as Viola Plummer, one of the marchers. How did these cops know the protestors? They certainly weren't anonymous.

The answer was astonishing. Chimurenga, Wareham, Plummer, and the others were part of a group known as "The New York 8," both to the NYPD and to the media. In fact, this group was well known to the NYPD because the Intelligence Division within the department had been monitoring their activities for some time. The monitoring had begun prior to the 1985 arrest of that group for plotting to rob the New York City Transit headquarters in Brooklyn, and it continued after many of them were acquitted of that charge but convicted of weapons possession in federal court in 1986. In fact, the monitoring had continued right up until a presentation the Intelligence Division conducted for the Brooklyn South Task Force, the police detachment assigned to work the demonstrations, the protests, and occasional riots. When the Intelligence Division's engrossing speaker was finished his presentation, every member of the Task Force knew Coltrane Chimurenga and the New York 8, and that made the cops more than a little concerned for what would happen that Saturday in July of 1987.[12]

The cops in the task force weren't the only ones concerned about the "Day of Outrage." Mayor Koch had decided to make a stand against the group and brought out the heavy artillery. On that day, Crown Heights had the appearance of an armed camp. Cops were everywhere as were police barriers. The community was afraid and not too many people braved the hot streets.

The protestors who did show up were professionals and not at all fazed by the army of cops, and the cops themselves were pretty bored because of the meager crowd. In police department vernacular it was "hurry up and wait" and a "dog and pony show," which was also referred to as "NYPD overkill." But one day the cops would look back fondly on those days of "overkill," such as in 1989 when they were being beaten back on the Brooklyn Bridge by an overwhelming crowd of protestors. But there would be other events in the interim.

Although the first "Day of Outrage" in 1987 met with unspectacular results, it did not dampen the enthusiasm and commitment of the black activists who organized it, especially Carson, Rev. Al Sharpton, Daughtry, and the activist lawyers Alton Maddon, Vernon Mason, and Colin Moore. This was not a homogeneous group and, as always with coalitions, there was a great deal of divergent opinion and conflicting strategic theory. But one thing could be counted on: If there was an incident that opened the door for renewed protest, then these activists would show up. Unfortunately, a criminal element in Bensonhurst provided that incident.

YUSUF HAWKINS

On August 24, 1989, Yusuf Hawkins, a young black kid, was shot by a Bensonhurst youth named Joey Fama, a kid with mob ties and a criminal record. The circumstances of the shooting and the dramatic and controversial aftermath have been documented in a book by John DeSantis, *Yusuf Hawkins, For the Color of His Skin*, a title that alludes to the racially motivated killing. Had the shooter acted alone and had it been any other neighborhood besides Bensonhurst, there might not have been as much political fallout. But Bensonhurst had long been on the radar of the black activists who regarded it as one of the most prejudiced neighborhoods in New York City.[13] Coming on the heels of the Howard Beach manslaughter convictions, Bensonhurst merely stirred the embers, and the flames of outrage easily reignited.

Within days of the shooting, Rev. Al Sharpton had embraced the victim's father, Moses Stewart, and began pushing the racial issues. Soon there were protest marches in Bensonhurst and elsewhere. The politics of confrontation were once again in full swing, and although most if not everyone in New York City empathized with the victim's family, the community of Bensonhurst remained defiant in the face of protest and scrutiny.

The Howard Beach case had set the tone two years earlier and established a pattern for both the defendants in the case and the protestors who came to the neighborhood in search of justice. The Yusuf Hawkins murder in one sense differed from the Michael Griffith (Howard Beach) manslaughter, but in another sense there were many similarities. Unlike Griffith, Hawkins was intentionally murdered or at least he died by a gunshot fired by one defendant, Joey Fama. Griffith had died because he had been hit by a car as he was chased by a mob of white kids. That is where the differences end and the similarities begin. Hawkins and Griffith were dead because they were black kids in a predominantly white neighborhood. Hawkins had been bothered, if not chased by a group of young white men before he was shot, and he had ventured into Bensonhurst, like Griffith in Howard Beach, for legitimate purposes. That did not matter to the white mob and it ultimately cost him his life.

The protest marches, especially those that took place in the heart of Bensonhurst, exposed some smoldering racial tensions and prompted intense, vitriolic rhetoric and activity on both sides of the issue. The black activists were protesting through the streets of an intensely protective if not chauvinistic Italian-American enclave in the heart of South Brooklyn, and the residents were not reticent in voicing their displeasure. What got lost in the confrontation was the real issue, the wasted life of Yusuf Hawkins, who by this time had become an icon for the protest. This is not to say that the black activists were at fault, but the people of Bensonhurst, especially the innocent ones, felt that they were being exploited by the activists and unfairly portrayed in the media as racist. Once again, their reactions and their public actions did little to convey any empathy they might have had for the victim and his family and only served to increase racial tensions. So the protest marches continued for the rest of August until a significant event occurred.

The Brooklyn Bridge Riot

On September 1, 1989, most of New York City was getting ready for the Labor Day weekend, which meant that the Thursday afternoon traffic took on the tone of a Friday. It was getaway day. But Sonny Carson and Coltrane Chimurenga had other ideas.

Another "Day of Outrage" was planned, a march from Grand Army Plaza on the periphery of Crown Heights, up Flatbush Avenue, and over the Brooklyn Bridge to City Hall, where the protestors would air their grievances for Mayor Koch. The timing of the march was a bit curious, coinciding with the beginning of an extended weekend and the end of the summer. It was a big traffic day, and the Brooklyn Bridge was always a traffic trouble spot. Historically, the bridge was a Brooklyn icon and consistently the stage for political protests that usually began in Brooklyn and ended up somewhere in Manhattan.

On this day, all the regular players were on hand and, as usual, a contingent from NYPD's Brooklyn South Task Force was present for the march. The task force had been ubiquitous at Sonny Carson and New York 8 protests. The Task Force commander, Lieutenant. Ray Powers, was conversant with Carson, Chimurenga, and the others, including Sharpton and Daughtry. They were practically on a first-name basis.

As the marchers made their way up Flatbush Avenue toward the bridge, the lead protestors were carrying two mock caskets draped in grey bunting. The caskets were symbolic of Yusuf Hawkins and Huey Newton, the former Black Panther who had also recently been killed in Oakland, California.[14] The caskets were also symbolic of Michael Griffith who died in Howard Beach, of Michael Stewart who died while being arrested in the subway in the early 1980s, and for all the victims of what the protestors called "white oppression."

What happened next became front-page news in the continuing saga of political confrontations. The protestors wanted to march on the vehicular roadway to Manhattan. There was a pedestrian walkway that most protests usually used, but the leaders of the march, especially Chimurenga, indicated that they were intent on marching on the roadway. They wanted to block the traffic. The #2 man in the NYPD, Chief of Patrol David Scott, himself a black man with at least 30 years' experience who had a working relationship with Carson, stood in front of a phalanx of Task Force cops blocking the entrance to the roadway on the Brooklyn Bridge. Scott and the cops were allowing the protestors to march over the pedestrian walkway. Chimurenga and his fellow lead marchers sauntered right up to Chief Scott and the cops. Chimurenga demanded to march through. Scott told him that he must go on the pedestrian walkway. Chimurenga said no and moved closer. According to a Task Force cop Brian Carey, who witnessed the confrontation, Scott and Chimurenga were "belly to belly," screaming at each other. Carey related, "Scott would not budge and Chimurenga and his crew kept pushing forward. It was very tense. Everyone knew there was going to be a fight but nobody expected this many people, and no one expected what happened next."

Carey continued his dramatic recollection:

> What happened next was the guys carrying the caskets opened the lids and produced a bunch of ax handles and wooden sticks and handed them out to the crowd of protestors. Everyone started swinging the ax handles and then bricks started flying. I was standing up on the wall of the Bridge and there was a guy above me on the walkway, swinging a brick inside a plastic bag. The brick kept hitting me in the head. I hit the guy with my night-stick and tried to grab him. A captain came over and grabbed me and told me I was getting too crazy and to go to the back of the line and cool off. So I did.

Carey didn't stay there long:

> I was there for a while until I saw a white guy swinging a camera and hitting cops in the head with it. He must have hit about three or four cops with it. He was knocking them down on the ground. I think he knocked one of them out. I couldn't stand it anymore so I tackled him. We both ended up on the front page of the Post. His name was Clayton Patterson and unbeknownst to me, he had made a name for himself in the Tompkins Square riots in 1988. Now he was somebody famous, but to me he was just an asshole swinging a camera and hurting cops. So I arrested him for assault and we both went to Central Booking.

Meanwhile the nightmare was continuing on the bridge. Other cops were also getting hit with bricks and bottles. Robert McFadden of the *New York Times* described the riotous scene in which 20 cops were injured and hospitalized:

> Night sticks flailed and bottles and bricks flew as the leading ranks of a predominantly black crowd of 7,500 demonstrators breached the police lines in an attempt to cross the bridge …
>
> Four people, including two photographers were arrested as the police kept the protestors off the bridges roadways.[15]

Because the Brooklyn Bridge riot happened at the beginning of the long Labor Day weekend, there were no major political repercussions aside from finger-pointing from both sides. The police had been assured by the protest organizers that the march would be peaceful and proceed over the pedestrian walkway. The protestors were angered by the riot gear worn by the cops and their tactics. Regardless, the tension had come to a head, although not for an extended period, and there had been some ugly violence. More protest was on the horizon.

The Korean Boycott

Fairly early in the mayoralty of David Dinkins, an incident occurred that was not only a harbinger of future conflict, but it would unfortunately set the tone for the next four years and greatly undermine his own political claims of being a "healer" for the city.

On January 18, 1990, a Haitian woman named Ghislaine Felissaint was shopping in the Red Apple Market, a fruit and vegetable store located at the corner of Church Avenue and St. Paul's Place in Flatbush, a mixed neighborhood with a large Haitian population. The store was owned and operated by a Korean man named Bong Jae Jung. At some point Felissaint and an employee of the store were entangled in a dispute. Felissaint landed on the floor and alleged that the Korean worker had assaulted her. Eventually, Bong Jae Jung was arrested and charged with assault, but was later acquitted owing to the fact that he had not been working on the day in question. But at the time of the incident, tensions had already been running hot in Brooklyn, and soon the Red Apple Market was the site of an intense, bitter, and protracted boycott.

Within days of the incident, Sonny Carson and a group of black activists descended on Church Avenue and began to picket in front of the store, intimidating potential customers and raising a general ruckus. The idea was to ruin the Korean's business. That is what boycotts usually intend to accomplish. Carson was no stranger to protest, and had initiated and participated in another boycott at a Korean store in Bedford-Stuyvesant in 1988. The modus operandi was the same in Flatbush. Carson and the protestors clamored for racial justice. The Korean owner, Jung, was arrested but the boycott continued.

Meanwhile Jung and his partner went to court and obtained an injunction against the picketers. In situations such as this, whether it is a union picketing a non-union store, or an informational picket like this one, a judge will typically set up some parameters for the pickets. These parameters are designed to accomplish a number of things. They help keep the peace while protecting both parties' constitutional rights. In Carson's case it was the right to freedom of expression. In the case of the Korean owners it was the right to conduct business without interference.

From the inception of the boycott, the NYPD had set up a permanent "detail" in the vicinity of the boycott, understanding the propensity for controversy and the potential for trouble. Following the judge's ruling, the Brooklyn South Task Force, which supplied manpower to the detail, put in place some protocols to enforce the judge's injunction. When one of the picketers crossed the line and violated the terms of the injunction, the police arrested the picketer. Very shortly after the arrest of the picketer, word was sent from City Hall to the Commanding Officer of the Task Force, Captain Ray Powers, that all incidents such as this would be referred to civil court. No criminal enforcement action was to be taken; no further arrests were to be made. According to Captain Powers, "In effect, our hands were tied. We ruined a lot of good cops on that detail, young guys and girls who were forced to stand around and watch people break the law and get away with it. It was an embarrassment."

For 19 months this continued until the criminal case was settled; Jung was acquitted by virtue of eye-witness testimony that he wasn't present at the time of the alleged assault, and also because the witness stated that the Fellissaint had thrown herself on the ground and was not assaulted by anyone. The civil suit continued, and for a time so did the boycott, but eventually the situation died down.

But in many ways, a great deal of damage had been done, not only to race relations in Brooklyn, but also to Dinkins and his administration's claims to heal the city. There was widespread criticism of the tactics used by the city and the perception of bias either against the Koreans or in favor of the black protestors. Dinkins' handling of the entire affair, and even the mayoral commission he had empanelled to investigate the situation, was questioned. In a memo from Deputy Mayor Bill Lynch, the damaging findings of the committee were evident in its Summary of Findings and Conclusions: "The appearance of potential bias of some Mayor's Committee members severely compromises the findings in the Report and its usefulness as an instrument to resolve the conflict."[16]

The report questioned the selections of Laura Blackburne and Karen Daughtry as committee members. Blackburne had been proposed by Dinkins for the position of chair for the New York City Housing Authority and, as such would appear to have a vested interest in a positive report for the mayor. Karen Daughtry was married to the Reverend Herbert Daughtry, the high-profile black community activist and himself one of the notable boycotters on Church Avenue. Taking this into account, Karen Daughtry's objectivity was greatly questioned. An even more questionable appointment was that of Wilson Desir, who stated publicly that he would try to have one of the stores closed permanently. The committee felt there was more than a perceived conflict of interest.[17]

Perhaps the most damning finding in the report is the one that underscored the problem that would arise a year later in Crown Heights:

> The Mayor's Committee's recommendations regarding the police are inappropriate and contrary to established law, as articulated by the Appellate Division. The police are charged with enforcing laws and court orders, which at times may involve confrontation. The Mayor's Committee's recommendation that confrontation be avoided because it may hinder the process of resolution depicts an erroneous view of the function of the police, and evidences a bias in favor of appeasement of the protestors at the expense of the rights of the store owners and the residents who wish to shop at the stores.[18]

This analysis cuts to the heart of the perception that Mayor Dinkins was a man who wanted to avoid confrontation, in some instances a laudable attitude. But in New York City politics, confrontation was a fact of life. The committee recognized that Dinkins had effectively tied the Police Department's hands, which seemed to play into the hands of the boycotters. This issue will never be conclusively settled but the perception in New York City was that Dinkins had encouraged the protestors, either intentionally or not, by repeatedly restraining the police from taking action. As a result, there was a series of confrontations that eventually led to the riot in Crown Heights. The activists had been emboldened by an indecisive response to many of their unlawful and, at times violent protests.

The latter half of the 1980s witnessed a series of tragic incidents that had an enormous impact on race relations in New York City. The Bernie Goetz shooting in 1985, followed by the death of Michael Griffith in Howard Beach in 1986. That event,which rekindled the perception of a racist neighborhood, prompted the first of many "Days of Outrage," and in 1987 a new controversial incident roiled the media and New York. The Tawana Brawley media circus served, for a while, as a cause célèbre for Reverend

Sharpton and the activist lawyers Mason, Maddox, and Moore. Brawley's story was exposed as a hoax and for a while it appeared that Sharpton's star might fade. The murder of Yusuf Hawkins brought Sharpton back into the center of the storm. By 1990, Brooklyn had seen numerous protests and marches, in Brooklyn North and in the South. The atmosphere was charged, the racial divide was widening, and the Korean boycott on Church Avenue certainly fanned the flames of contention.

THE SECRET RELATIONSHIP

In the summer of 1991 a couple of events from the world of academia served to turn up the heat on the boiling cauldron of racial politics in New York City. One of them was the release of notes and comments from a speech given by Professor Leonard Jeffries, the chair of Black Studies at City University of New York. The speech was covered by the *New York Post*, which broke the story. Jeffries made headlines with this statement on July 20, 1991 at the Empire State Black Arts and Cultural Festival in Albany, New York:

> Jeffries asserted that "rich Jews" controlled the Black slave trade, and that Hollywood was the site of a Jewish-dominated conspiracy to systematically denigrate Blacks. He called then Assistant U.S. Secretary of Education Diane Ravitch the "ultimate, supreme, sophisticated, debonair racist" and a "Texas Jew.[19]

His comments about the slave trade echoed another controversial development from academia. The Nation of Islam Historical Research Department published a book entitled *The Secret Relationship Between Blacks and Jews.*[20] A well written, exhaustively researched, and academically structured work, the book went to great lengths to document that the African slave trade was dominated by Jews, almost from its inception:

> But this is not the only charge that is made against Jews. Jews have been conclusively linked to the greatest criminal endeavor ever undertaken against an entire race of people—a crime against humanity—the Black African Holocaust. They were participants in the entrapment and forcible exportation of millions of Black African citizens into the wretched and inhuman life of bondage for the financial benefit of Jews. The effects of this unspeakable tragedy are still being felt among the peoples of the world at this very hour.
>
> Deep within the recesses of the Jewish historical record is the irrefutable evidence that the most prominent of the Jewish pilgrim fathers used

kidnapped Black Africans disproportionately more than any other ethnic group or religious group in New World history and participated in every aspect of the international slave trade.

Most have always assumed that the relationship between blacks and Jews has been mutually supportive, friendly and fruitful—two suffering people bonding to overcome hatred and bigotry to achieve success. But history tells an altogether different story.

Rabbi Henry Cohen, author of the book, *Justice Justice*, makes a telling point.

The parallels between Nazi terror and the American slave trade are more startling than we may realize.[21]

A perfunctory reading of this work would give the appearance that there was documented historical evidence of the title's premise, but closer scrutiny of the annotations and attributions indicated that not a lot of new ground had been broken. Indeed, there had always been historical documentation of Jews' complicity with other white men in the African slave trade because it was a fact of history. What was being alleged in the *Secret Relationship* was the Jews' prominence in said practice. The assertion was that Jews instituted the African slave trade and were disproportionately its greatest practitioners. It is apparent that this is not the case. Jews were involved in the African slave trade in proportionate numbers to their representation in society and international business.

The book and the accompanying controversy set a blaze in academic circles, especially in the Jewish community, which long considered itself a kindred spirit with the black community because of a common history of oppression and persecution. The publishing of *The Secret Relationship* by the Nation of Islam was not a shock to the Jewish community, but it did represent one more crack in the already-crumbling liberal Jewish–black coalition. Testimony to that deteriorating relationship was everywhere, from the black nationalistic rhetoric of Elijah Muhammad and Malcolm X in the early 1960s to the Ocean Hill-Brownsville school district protest in 1968. The Nation of Islam had put Jews on notice as early as the 1950s and some in the Jewish liberal community had recognized it.[22]

The Nation of Islam's theory has been refuted in another comprehensive historical work written by in 1998 by Eli Faber called *Jews, Slaves and the Slave Trade: Setting the Record Straight*.[23] Faber used the words of black academia's most prolific voices to confront the theories of the Nation of Islam when he quoted Henry Louis Gates, Jr.:

> Henry Louis Gates, Jr. characterized the *Secret Relationship Between Blacks and Jews* as "the Bible of the new anti-Semitism." As such the volume represented a new if not wholly original contribution to the corpus of anti-Semitic ideas. To the litany of Christ killer, well poisoner, userer, unscrupulous businessman, ruthless banker, conspirator bent on world domination and racial polluter was now added the label of slave trader.[24]

According to Faber, the Nation of Islam work was also viewed skeptically within the rest of the academic world:

> In the public controversy that ensued after publication of the *Secret Relationship Between Blacks and Jews*, the Council of the American Historical Association, the organization's elected governing board, adopted a resolution in which it labeled as false any statement alleging that Jews played a disproportionate role in the exploitation of slave labor or in the Atlantic Slave Trade.[25]

In a vigorous defense of Jews against the charges leveled by the Nation of Islam, Faber cites innumerable instances where Jews themselves were the subject of discrimination and persecution in Europe, especially during the years when the African slave trade was a profitable activity for burgeoning nations like England, Spain, and Portugal, nations that had exiled Jews from their borders. It is clear from Faber's narrative and analysis that Jews were not only reviled in some circles in Europe, but that the trend continued on the other side of the Atlantic in the West Indies and Brazil.[26]

Aside from the accusations hurled back and forth, and the defense of Jews in the slave trade, what remained a constant through history was the tenuous position of Jews in Eastern Europe, Western Europe, and then in the New World. Reasons for this status have been the fuel for endless speculation throughout modern times. Professor John O'Brien of Queens College has attempted to understand and perhaps explain this phenomenon by describing the Jews as a "non-conforming minority of exceptional cohesion." His terminology focuses on the uniqueness of the Jewish religion as the original monotheistic religion and the resultant persecution Jews suffered at the hands of nearby antagonists. Whether the persecutions were in response to this monotheism or maybe a combination of factors that include basic geographical battles, racial and ethnic differences, or other socioeconomic factors doesn't seem to matter now. What happened to the Jews was the development of anti-Semitism. And this may be the most essential fact of their separateness in modern times.

Anti-Semitism was the prime consideration for Josef Schneerson when he brought the Lubavitcher world headquarters to America and to Crown Heights, as it was for most Jews who were escaping persecution in Europe. That persecution had been a constant source of misery for Jews since medieval times, especially during the Crusades and again when they were the targets of the Spanish Inquisition. This history of persecution followed the Jews to America, where anti-Semitism also took hold. One of the new practitioners of American anti-Semitism were members of the Nation of Islam under the leadership of Elijah Muhammad.

The Nation of Islam

The leader of the Brooklyn Bridge Day of Outrage, the man who stood "belly to belly" against the Chief of Patrol of the New York City Police Department, Coltrane Chimurenga, had been affiliated with the Nation of Islam. Chimurenga had been educated at Harvard University, where he had been working toward a doctorate. But Chimurenga's real education had taken place on the streets of New York when he went by the name Randolph Simms, and in its courtrooms, when he was later tried for various crimes, including conspiracy to break into an upstate prison to free a prisoner and also to commit robberies.[27] Chimurenga and his group, called at the time The Revolutionary Communist Military Command, were acquitted of the conspiracy charges but convicted of numerous weapons possession charges. Later on, because of the trial, the group came to be known as the New York 8 and included other highly educated black revolutionaries. They also were known as the December 12th Movement, and had dedicated themselves to the support of a revolution in America.

The Nation of Islam was founded by Robert J. Poole, who took the name Elijah Muhammad after receiving visionary instructions from Master W. Fard Muhammad, who appeared to Poole as Allah or God. Poole had moved his family from Macon, Georgia to Detroit. It was there that Elijah Muhammad became engrossed in this movement, converting to Islam and delving into the mission of the Nation of Islam, which was the salvation of the black race, both spiritually and temporally. But the Islam that Elijah Muhammad and his followers practiced was called Bilalian Islam, and diverged at times sharply from the mainstream. One of the key differences was Elijah Muhammad's own claims to be "the Prophet," which is heresy in traditional Islam. Bilalianism also avows that God or Allah is Black and adheres to a policy of black supremacy. In Bilalian Islam Whites are characterized as evil.[28]

Elijah Muhammad's message to the black men and women of America was one of self-determination and rejection of the white man's imposed societal constraints. Eventually Elijah Muhammad would lead the Nation of Islam as it amassed a larger membership of converts to its unique form of Islam. In the late 1950s and early 1960s, two new leaders would surface within the movement, Malcolm X, formerly Malcolm Little, who had been converted in prison, and Louis Farrakhan (X), who was an early protégé of Malcolm X and later, after the death of Elijah Muhammad, assumed leadership of the Nation. These two controversial figures have been harshly criticized over the years for their public espousal of anti-Semitism. Although it was Farrakhan who attracted a huge public outcry for anti-Semitic statements in the late 1980s and 1990s, it was Malcolm X who shocked a relatively naive American public with his overt anti-Semitism and what was perceived at the time as racism in reverse. In his book *Black Leadership*, Marable Manning detailed a highly controversial meeting between Malcolm X and leaders of the Klu Klux Klan:

> On January 28, 1961, Malcolm X and Jeremiah X, the minister of the Atlanta mosque, met with leaders of the KKK. Unknown to both parties, however, the FBI was present, and the agency secretly recorded the discussion. The Nation's representatives and the Klansmen first shared their views on race and quickly found common ground. Malcolm X reportedly attributed "the whole struggle to a Jewish conspiracy carried out by unsuspecting Blacks.[29]

Revelations such as these were shocking to not only the American public, but had broad repercussions in the liberal community, especially the liberal Jewish community, a group that had served an integral part in the early Civil Rights Movement. The early Freedom Riders" included a diverse group of black and white activists who were committed to civil rights. But the tone of the movement was changing in the mid 1960s, as the nonviolent approach espoused by the Rev. Martin Luther King Jr. gave way to the political and sometimes violent confrontations advocated by some in the Nation of Islam and later groups such as the Black Panthers, the Black Liberation Army, and the group led by Coltrane Chimurenga, the December 12th Movement.

The early years of the Civil Rights Movement were far from peaceful, but the determination evinced by Reverend King, Jr. infused the movement with intestinal fortitude. King's commitment to nonviolence was an essential cornerstone to the movement and, as King proclaimed, was proof that the black man was indeed on the righteous path: "We proved that we possessed the most formidable weapon of all—the conviction that we were right. We had the protection of our knowledge that we were more concerned about realizing our righteous aims than about saving our skins."[30]

King himself felt that the idea of nonviolence would underscore this righteousness and convince the American public that civil rights was most certainly a just cause:

> The Negro's method of non-violent direct action is not only suitable as a remedy for injustice; its very nature is such that it challenges the myth of inferiority. Even the most reluctant are forced to recognize that no inferior people could choose and successfully pursue a course involving such extensive sacrifice, bravery and skill.[31]

But King's assassination on April 4, 1968 in Memphis only served to bring about the violence he had feared was dangerously close to the surface back in 1963:

> In the summer of 1963 the knife of violence was just that close to the nation's aorta. Hundreds of cities might now be mourning countless dead but for the operation of certain forces which gave political surgeons an opportunity to cut boldly and safely remove the deadly peril.[32]

The nonviolence of King's "direct action" gave way to the confrontational politics of the Nation of Islam, Malcolm X, and Louis Farrakhan. By the late 1960s the streets of the inner city were racked with violence and crime. Riots broke out in almost all the major cities in the United States, all of them about race and civil rights. Gone were the relatively peaceful but forceful protests of the Freedom Rides, replaced with an angry, new group of activists. A target of this new leadership was the Jews, who were looked on as a group that exploited the black man. One of those young activists was Sonny Carson who explained the transformation in his philosophy:

> Suddenly, one gentleman, a very high official in the principals' association objected to our attitude and began to berate us. If I recall, his theme was that he was here to help The Community, he being Jewish and also being an underdog. And before he could continue, one of our members interrupted him and said, "Whenever it benefits you Jews, you come up with that brotherhood crap."[33]

Carson's recollection reinforces what many political scientists and observers had been recognizing as "anti-Semitism in the Ghetto." Whether these ideas had been brought about by Nation of Islam rhetoric or were simply the result of personal experience, it became a fact of life that there was a great deal of resentment for the Jew in the urban black neighborhoods, or ghettoes, as the term was often misused. It was also obvious that Carson, Chimurenga, and the New York 8 espoused the views and strategies of the radical Nation of Islam. This new and perhaps surprising anti-Semitism was one of the key points of Max Geltman's *The Confrontation: Black Power, Anti-Semitism and the Myth of Integration*. Geltman recognized this new dilemma and the inherent danger for the Jew in urban America, and the quote bears repeating:

"One may deduce that, although Jewish boys and girls were in the vanguard of those 'going to Mississippi,' the Jew is now in the unpleasant and dangerous position of scapegoat for the Negro. As before, there will be no one to protect him [the Jew]."[34]

In 1970 Geltman (and many others) understood the problems plauging urban America, both as a result of the riot-beset late 1960s, and looking toward where the issues were headed:

> Despite the efforts of certain well-meaning Jewish spokesmen, the Jews in this country may be in for a very hard time just because the Negro sees them both [Jews and Whites] as exploiters and as benefactors. This dual identification was visible in Germany before the holocaust, when the Jew was denounced as both Communist and capitalist in the same breath. To the Negro in the American city today the Jew is as visible as is the Negro to the white community as a whole.[35]

Although Geltman's analysis was by no means prophetic, he succinctly identified and described a growing anti-Semitism in the black ghetto. These feelings had been developing since the late 1950s with the rise of the Nation of Islam and grew stronger through the riots that followed. It became increasingly evident in New York, especially during the Ocean Hill-Brownsville School District fiasco, which pitted former allies, the liberal Jewish United Federation of Teachers against the black and Hispanic parents and students of that community. It was more painfully illustrated to Albert Shanker during the antagonistic negotiations of that period. There were many times when Shanker was thankful to leave the community meetings with his hide intact. As Sonny Carson recalled: "Finally someone beckoned to the brothers at the door and they stepped aside and he was no longer confronted. This was the last time we were to see Mr. Shanker in The Black Community on his own."[36]

As Albert Shanker walked out that door, somewhere in Brooklyn the handwriting was on the wall. The old alliances were over, things had changed. The nonviolent protest of Martin Luther King Jr. in the 1960s had given way to the politics of confrontation of the Nation of Islam and its many tentacles, and in turn, there was a new manifestation in the streets of Brooklyn and the streets of Crown Heights. "The Days of Outrage" of the late 1980s served notice on the community that there was an incendiary element in society, an element that was looking for a spark. Robert Singh recognized and analyzed this "changing of the guard" in black activism, and comments on the disparity in *The Farrakhan Phenomenon: Race, Reaction and the Paranoid Style in American Politics*:

> The historic public and private divisions between the non-violent, principally southern based struggle for multi-racial unity and integration personified by King and Malcolm X's aggressive, and predominantly northern urban militant black separatism were deep and almost by definition, unreconcilable.[37]

By all appearances it seemed that this dynamic was at work in New York City in the late 1980s onward. David Dinkins, campaigning as a "healer," seemed to subscribe to the King philosophy, while Sonny Carson and his cohorts in the New York 8 seemed to be decidedly in the Farrakhan-Nation of Islam camp. Somewhere in the middle were the activist preachers Daughtry and Sharpton. They advocated protest and confrontation but not necessarily violence. But if politics made for strange bedfellows so did political and racial activism.

As we have seen, the Days of Outrage targeted a number of communities, and the reverend activists Sharpton and Daughtry had been leading marches for years in Bedford-Stuyvesant and elsewhere in Brooklyn. While Carson, Chimurenga, and the New York 8 had one agenda, the reverend activists had another. Perhaps the agendas were similar, but the methods differed. Many times over the years, however, their paths would converge. The Brooklyn Bridge was one place and the Korean Boycott on Church Avenue in Flatbush was another. In the next to last week of August 1991, their protest paths would cross once again, this time in Crown Heights.

CHAPTER 9

RAY POWERS

Raymond T. Powers is a retired Deputy Chief of the New York City Police Department. The rank of Deputy Chief is the third-highest rank in the NYPD and obviously comes with enormous responsibility. At the time of his retirement, Ray Powers was the commanding officer of the Operations Division, a unit responsible for everything that goes on in New York City. As commander of the Operations Division, Powers directly supervised a large contingent of officers, including an Inspector, a Deputy Inspector, a Captain, many Lieutenants, even more Sergeants, and squads of police officers who man the myriad stations within the vast two-floor Command and Control Center inside police headquarters in downtown Manhattan.

Prior to his promotion to Commanding Officer of the Operations Division, Powers had been the Commanding Officer of the 67th Precinct, located in the Flatbush section of South Brooklyn. In a career that spanned four decades, Ray Powers worked his way up from Patrolman in the Bronx through the Brooklyn South Narcotics Division and was then promoted to Sergeant, where he supervised patrol in Brooklyn North. In 1984 he was promoted to Lieutenant and soon after was assigned as the Commanding Officer of the Brooklyn South Task Force. At the time Powers was 36 years old and was considered to be a "rising star." According to those in the know, this had as much to do with Powers' ability and competence as it had to do with his ability to relate to people and deal with problems. For the Police Department he was a problem solver. At the time of the Crown Heights riots in 1991 Powers, then a Captain, was the Executive Officer of the 70th Precinct in the Parkville section of South Brooklyn, which covers a large swath of land along Ocean Avenue, north to and including Prospect Park, east to Bedford Avenue where it borders the 67th Precinct (for many years the most dangerous and deadly precinct in Brooklyn South), and south to what is called the Junction at Flatbush Avenue and Nostrand Avenue. Brooklyn College is located in the Junction. In

Brooklyn's heyday, the Junction was (and remains) a bustling and vibrant transit hub and commercial shopping district.

Ray Powers knew Brooklyn South as well as any captain or high-ranking officer in the command, owing to his years as the Commanding Officer of the Brooklyn South Task Force. The Task Force conducts patrols in the entire borough and is utilized to police any significant problem. There is a task force for each borough command in New York City, which means there was at the time of the riot in 1991 a task force in the Bronx, Manhattan South and Manhattan North, Brooklyn South and Brooklyn North, Queens, and Staten Island. (The larger boroughs in the city are divided into two parts to facilitate effective management.) The task forces were the descendants of the old Tactical Patrol Force, or TPF, which was legendary throughout the 60s and 70s for its effect on rough neighborhoods that were experiencing higher crime and/or violent activities, including riots. The word was that TPF was a unit that you didn't want to mess with. Working out of a central command office, the men of TPF were usually dispatched for weeks at a time to various precincts that needed special attention. According to legend, when TPF came to a precinct, it was not a happy time to be a criminal or potential bad guy.

By the late 1970s TPF was disbanded and some of the old legions now formed the various task forces. But it was common knowledge in the late 1980s that the task force was nothing compared to TPF. Word had it that TPF was disbanded because Mayor Lindsay didn't like the idea of it. Regardless, the new task forces were essentially expected to perform some of the TPF duties, especially responding to riot situations.

Ray Powers commanded the Brooklyn South Task Force from 1985 until 1990. Those five years were some of the most controversial and contentious times in Brooklyn, north or south. And as we have seen, they were trying times for New York City in general. That period saw the 1985 Bernard Goetz shooting of five unarmed black teenagers on a subway train and the 1986 "lynching" of Michael Griffith, an unarmed black man who was walking through the neighborhood of Howard Beach on a Friday night. Coming across the "wrong crowd," Griffith was chased, because he was a black man in a white neighborhood, and he ran onto the Belt Parkway where he was struck by a car and killed. In 1989 Yusuf Hawkins was shot and killed by a group of white Italian-American kids in Bensonhurst, Brooklyn. Once again race was a determining factor in the violence.[1] Each of these incidents had a profound effect on the community and was punctuated by a great deal of irate protest by the black community, which had a variety of leaders including Rev. Herbert Daughtry and Rev. Al Sharpton; the black activist attorneys Alton Maddox, C. Vernon Mason, and Colin Moore; Sonny Carson and his ally, the New York 8; and others.[2]

Many of those protest marches were held in Brooklyn, especially Brooklyn South. As a result, Lieutenant Ray Powers and his Brooklyn South Task Force could usually be found in the middle of these demonstrations. Powers was a hands-on, proactive commander. Very often Powers could be found marching right alongside the protestors, sometimes even in their midst, often conversing with the leaders in an effort to keep the channels of communication open. As one might suspect, this type of activity often put Powers and his task force in the eye of the storm, but it also garnered much respect for his work ethic and personal integrity. This was the sentiment on both sides of the street. The protestors gave him grudging respect, and the cops who worked for him were extremely loyal. It was a well-known fact that Powers would not ask a cop to do something that he himself would not do; without fail, Ray Powers was standing side-by-side with his cops taking care of business and even sometimes taking a beating. It has often been said of a well-respected cop that he was "a cop's cop." Powers was exactly that, but he was also, quintessentially, "a cop's boss." He took care of his men but he also demanded a lot.

On Monday evening, August 19, 1991, Powers was at home in Long Island when his phone rang. It was the Brooklyn South Borough command calling to tell him that a disturbance was ongoing in the 71st Precinct. To Powers this came as no surprise. He had spent years in Crown Heights following Sonny Carson and Coltrane Chimurenga and the rest of the New York 8 as they protested and raised a ruckus about inequity, inequality, and downright racist practices. At times Powers had commented that some of their gripes were more than legitimate. He was also well acquainted with Mendel Shemtov, Schmuel Blutmen, and the other Hasidic leaders who often were on the other side of the police barriers that Powers and his men set up. So when he got the news, Powers wasn't surprised. What did surprise him was that he wasn't called in on Monday night. As he termed it, "They [the borough command] felt that they had things under control. They were wrong."

Powers reported on Tuesday morning to the 71st and began doing what he did best: He organized the task force that would be needed to quell the growing disturbance. According to Powers it was not yet considered a riot: "Riots usually least four days. One day to find out it's a riot and then two days of severe violence followed by one day when things are finally brought under control." According to Powers it was "a haphazard mobilization on Tuesday." (A mobilization is police jargon for assigning police officers to a location where a disturbance is occurring. In the NYPD there are various stages, or levels of mobilization. By the time Crown Heights was burning they had reached the highest level, but did not initially start there.) Powers said that it took some time to organize the mobilization on Tuesday, but by Wednesday it was being managed much better. The Girgenti Commission Report, commissioned by Governor Mario Cuomo after the riot, was highly critical of the organization and tactics of the police at the inception of the riot, citing Assistant Chief Thomas Gallagher, the Commanding Officer of Brooklyn North, as not being hard enough on the rioters early. Powers disagrees with that assessment, stating that Gallagher had told him in no uncertain terms to "Stop it! Stop it now, Ray."

Tuesday evening, August 20, a light rain was falling as Powers and his task force were attempting to march up Utica Avenue from Empire Boulevard to Eastern Parkway. It is a rather steep hill and there was a great deal of rioting and looting going on toward the high end of the street near Eastern Parkway. At one point, still near the bottom of the hill on the upward climb, a fire truck appeared and was trying to make its way up the street. Powers asked the fire lieutenant where he was headed and was told there was a fire in a building on Utica between President and Union streets. Powers, commending the Firemen for bravery, told them to follow the task force, which was on foot, and they would clear the way for the FD truck. Soon the battle was coming closer and suddenly Powers went down to the ground, struck in the groin and leg by a broken half of a brick. According to Powers, "That broke the tension. A few of the guys were laughing and as soon as I could, I was laughing a little, too. Now we started to move and soon we had the crowd headed out the other way. The FD guys got to the fire and we made our way to the sneaker store that was being looted."

This sneaker store, located on Eastern Parkway off Utica, is one of many focal points in Girgenti's report. There is a contradiction here. An officer interviewed by the commission stated that there was widespread looting at the store and no police action was taken. In fact, the officer, who is not named in the report, said that "superior officers at the scene told their subordinates to stand fast and not to break ranks. He believed there were more than enough police to form arrest teams, but any officer who moved, he said, was threatened with suspension. As a result, he said, they stood by and watched the store get looted."[3]

Ray Powers disputes that statement and, in fact, says he ordered many cops to go into the store and make arrests. In his own recollection he remembers saying, "There was no way that they [the cops] would be able to stand by and watch this happen."

It is important to remember that while this was going on, there were many Jewish residents cowering inside their homes, in apartment buildings on President Street and other spots throughout the area. The Girgenti Report reveals a disturbing series of calls to the 911 operator from a terrified Hasidic woman around 5 p.m. The woman is nearly hysterical as she begged the operator to send the police. The following snippet of this series of calls is extremely unnerving:

At 5:09 p.m. she again called, this time reporting that shots were being fired:

Caller: *yes. They are ... the black are rioting. They're on my street. They gotta gun. They shot two shots. I am not gonna live like this. Please get the police here*

911 Operator: *What's the address there?*

Caller: *—..., it's corner of Utica and President. We're in between Rochester and Utica.*

911 Operator: *What's your last name?*

Caller: *I'm not gonna say.*

911 Operator: *OK. Anybody hurt?*

Caller: *No. I don't know. They're breaking glass. I got two shots-two gun shots.*

911 Operator: *Two gun shots are flying?*

Caller: *What? I gotta house full of children, ma'am. I am shaking. What d'you want from me? Just please send the police here, it's a riot.*

911 Operator: *Ok the police are on the way, OK?*

In all she called 911 six times between 5:09 p.m. and 5:12 p.m., but the police did not come."[4]

Meanwhile, all hell was breaking loose in the immediate area. When the group of cops that Powers had been commanding reached the top of the hill, they found a fire on Utica Avenue and looting at the Sneaker King sneaker store. Debris, rocks, and bottles were flying through the air, forcing Powers to constantly bob and weave. As a matter of fact, Powers was relieved near dawn on Wednesday morning and had to laugh when his relief captain asked him why he was still ducking and weaving, because he was now standing inside the safety of the precinct. Bobbing and weaving, Powers walked back to his office and got some much-needed sleep.

Wednesday, August 21, 1991

By early Wednesday afternoon, Powers was already on his way back to the 71st Precinct, having been awakened by the Brooklyn South borough command beseeching him to return sooner than his relief time. Ever the good soldier, Powers had already planned to go early, and soon he was back on the street, once again bobbing and weaving.

But Wednesday presented new challenges and problems. Mayor Dinkins had decided to visit the area and hold a press conference from P.S. 167, which was in the immediate vicinity of the riot area, which was widening. Powers had also figured out a more efficient method of organizing and mobilizing the cops who were in the area. Powers determined that the cops did not know where to report and remedied the situation by designing some signs that directed them to their respective mobilization points. Once they knew where to report, the mobilization was more orderly, and as a result, a lot more effective.

By this time, late afternoon on Wednesday, commissioner Lee Brown's car was en route to P.S. 167 to meet the mayor and hold the press conference. Powers recalls the radio call of "Car One, 10-13," which Powers knew to be the commissioner's car. Things had hit rock bottom as the police commissioner was under siege and the mayor's car wouldn't be able to arrive because the area was so unstable.

One of the critiques of the NYPD's riot response was the inability to organize and control the rioters. The Girgenti Report and others criticized the police command and control, noting that chaos and disorganization were the order of the day. Powers recalls a situation in front of P.S. 167 that underscores that claim. According to Powers, the Inspector in charge of the mayor's security detail ordered Powers to get his men inside the school and secure it so that when the mayor arrived things would be in order. Powers complied and ordered a lot of cops inside the back door of the school, while rocks and bottles were still pelting the front. But soon, the Chief of Patrol Mario Selvaggi, himself only three days into his new job, showed up and screamed at Powers to get outside the school and take care of the rioters who were going crazy. Selvaggi accused Powers of cowardice in front of the cops and ordered them all outside. Powers tried to tell Selvaggi that he had been ordered by another supervisor to control the school. Selvaggi didn't want to hear it and continued to rail at Powers in front of everyone. Perhaps this moment crystallized the problems that were occurring; nobody had taken command, at least nobody of the highest ranks.

Selvaggi's appearance was curiously close to the arrival of the mayor at P.S. 167. Up to that point, he had been involved but not highly visible. Prior to this scene, Assistant Chief Gallagher had been commanding and coordinating. But now all the chiefs were on the scene, probably because the Police Commissioner and the mayor were soon to converge on the school.

But elsewhere in Crown Heights there were scenes similar to the one described by the Hasidic woman's call to 911. The streets south of Eastern Parkway were a battleground. By nightfall there were hundreds, if not thousands, of black rioters causing trouble, turning over cars, lighting them on fire, and smashing windows of what they perceived to be Jewish residences.

During this period, Captain Joe Esposito, one day destined to become the Chief of the NYPD, had devised a method of attacking this problem. Loading police vans with cops, the vans would back down the block, all the while being pelted by debris. The crowd of looters wasn't aware of what would happen next. The van would stop and the cops would pile out, chasing some of the rioters down the street and arresting others, throwing them in the van. Powers was in another van doing the same thing. Some of the front-line commanders were now taking care of business and the tide was beginning to turn.

"This was a talented group of commanders, captains, and managers," Powers later related. He continued, "They knew what to do and when they had the mandate to do it, things started to change. If you look at the people who worked in Brooklyn South at that time and where they wound up, it is pretty indicative of the quality: Joe Esposito became Chief of Department; Neil Dever, Chief of Brooklyn South; Ray Powers, C.O. of Operations; Vinnie Kennedy, Inspector and C.O. of Highway; Joe Cuneen became the Chief of Brooklyn North and the list goes on."

"A WHOLE 'NOTHER LEVEL"

– Deputy Mayor Bill Lynch, describing the situation he discovered in Crown Heights.

Apparently what was also needed for these quality commanders to be successful in controlling the riot was cooperation from the upper echelon of the Police Department and from the mayor himself. Evidently it took a chaotic and dangerous situation at P.S. 167 to hammer this idea home to the mayor and the police commissioner; Crown Heights was under siege and mere "healing" rhetoric would not do anything. Deputy Mayor Bill Lynch's description of these events supports this idea:

> On the way out [to P.S. 167], I'm in the car. I'm on the phone and we get on Eastern Parkway and the place is blocked off. To me police [were] everywhere. I'm wondering what's happening and what has happened is a group of kids had come through past the school running, threw rocks, bottles at reporters that were at the school and they wouldn't let the Mayor through. That's ... That concerned me deeply. I ... They held the Mayor up. I went through, down to the school and, you know, there had been some reporters who had been hit by rocks and bottles and to me that took it to a whole 'nother level. I had now, you know, seen this thing. It's Wednesday and that gets me really in focus.[5]

Perhaps the danger of P.S. 167 and his inability to hold a meaningful press conference prompted the mayor to give his street commanders a mandate to stop the riot. Maybe it was the "10-13" [officer needs assistance] call from "Car One," the police commissioner's car, that woke these leaders up to the fact that, if they were in this kind of trouble, what was happening to the common folk living in the neighborhood? People were calling 911 and begging for help from the police, begging the mayor to call out the National Guard. Many of these people were Jewish, Hasidic, Lubavitchers who had fled the "pogroms" of Europe and the concentration camps of World War II only to find themselves curled up behind tables and barricades inside their houses as an angry mob tried and sometimes succeeded in breaking down their doors.[6]

But it wasn't only Hasidic Jews who were afraid of the violence and mayhem occurring in their neighborhood, on their streets, and in their hallways. The black citizens of Crown Heights were also terrified and fed up with the lack of control in their neighborhood. The Girgenti Report cites numerous 911 calls from local black residents asking for some kind of police response to quell the violence. The transcripts of these calls illustrate the feeling of helplessness and frustration on the part of both the callers and the 911 operators who were in their offices fielding these calls and knowing there was little they could do besides attempt to calm the people down.

Indeed, a call to the 911 operator on Tuesday night supports this:

> **Caller:** *Yeah, um there are some guys ... stoning Jews on the corner of Lexington? ... stoning the Jews!*
>
> **911:** *What are they doing? They're stoning the Jews?*
>
> **Caller:** *Yes! They're throwing a lot of stones at the Jews.*
>
> **911:** *This is on Lexington? And what?*
>
> **Caller:** *Lexington between Troy and Albany.*
>
> **911:** *Do you have an address?*
>
> **Caller:** *No I ain't giving you my address ... flinging all the stones in the Jews' windows. That's you know ...*[7]

Another Dynamic

This is also supported anecdotally by many cops who were on the scene and by Ray Powers:

> There was another dynamic at work in Crown Heights. You had the Jews, the Blacks, the Cops and don't forget the other dynamic, the Caribbean Blacks. They held themselves as different from the American Black community."

> Powers continued, carefully choosing his words, "There was a perception within the Caribbean community that the American Blacks weren't as interested in working and investing in the community, buying homes and other things."

Powers said that he told many of the cops during the riot that many of the people in the community were not necessarily the enemy. To the contrary, they were the cops' friends. His recollection is telling, "On Wednesday afternoon, many cops were being treated to iced tea and water and soda by the residents of President Street and other blocks as well. I know from my experience, all the time I spent during the marches and protests over the years, that these were primarily West Indian people with a smaller amount of American Blacks as well."

Powers contends that many of the rioters, if not the majority, came from Brooklyn North and were part of the contingent that had been stirring up trouble during the marches led by Sonny Carson and the New York 8. He related, "The people who were rioting in the South were from the North. That was proved on Wednesday with the arrests that were made." As a lieutenant and later a captain in the Brooklyn South Task Force, Powers had followed and escorted these protest marchers through the streets of the 77th precinct [which is in Brooklyn North Command] and the 71st precinct. As early as 1986 Powers had occasion to meet and negotiate with Carson, Chimurenga, Daughtry, Sharpton, and other activists. Much of this activism was borne of the Howard Beach situation and continued later in Bensonhurst. Through all this, Powers maintains one important principle: "We always took care of the local neighborhood people. We [the Brooklyn South Task Force] helped Dr. Nichols get his car out on Saturday mornings. We helped people get into St. Mark's Church when there were crowds all around it. Sometimes we had to help the local black people navigate through the throngs of Hasidim on the street as the black people were also trying to get to church."

But Ray Powers is also a realist, "In politics somebody has to be a scapegoat to get somebody else off the hook." To Powers that scapegoat was Chief Tom Gallagher and the men and women of the NYPD in general. Powers realized this early on and felt that in all the postmortems that no one of any political significance was cited for ineptitude or malfeasance. But in the Girgenti Report Gallagher appears to be that scapegoat. Powers complained, "They ruined Tom Gallagher's reputation. And it was a good reputation earned over 30 years of quality work in the Police Department. He wanted that riot stopped on Tuesday afternoon and he told me in no uncertain terms to 'Stop it.' I knew what he wanted, but he also knew there weren't enough men. And he had very little control over that."

"You have to remember," Powers continued, "that Johnston [the long-time Chief of Department] had just retired on the previous Friday and now we had a new Chief of Department, David Scott who was on vacation. We had a new Chief of Patrol, Selvaggi, who was new to the situation, and we had a new chief of Brooklyn North in Benny Foster. Things were chaotic because of this and the fact that Lee Brown was where?" Powers answered his own question with the Commissioner's nickname given to him by the rank and file, "Out of town Brown."

"I do remember that Ray Kelly [the First Deputy Commissioner, a man who commanded a lot of respect within the department and also had a lot of experience in Crown Heights, himself being the former commanding officer of the 71st Precinct seven years earlier] was out there working behind the scenes." Powers recalled a situation early on Wednesday night when Utica had been blocked off to vehicular traffic, "I saw this black Jeep coming up Utica and I yelled to the cop that nobody was allowed up the street. The cop motioned to me by tapping his shoulder, the universal police sign that it was some sort of boss. When the car pulled up to me the windows were tinted and I couldn't see inside. But then the window rolled down, the occupant yelled over to me, 'Hey, Ray, how are you doing out here?' It was Kelly."

But the fact that Kelly was out on the street didn't greatly alter the fact that there was a vacuum of leadership at the top. Kelly's quote was broadcast on the all-news WINS radio report, "Nobody asked me."

The mistakes of Tuesday and Wednesday were largely overcome on Thursday by a greater influx of fresh cops and a reinvigorated and empowered management group. The strategy and tactics of Inspector Dever, and Captains Esposito and Powers had served to dishearten the rabble-rousers, and increased arrests and enforcement turned the tide of violence. By Friday morning Crown Heights was an armed camp, with clusters of police officers on every corner and mobile patrols with vanloads of cops on the look-out for troublemakers. It took four days but finally the mayor, the politicians, the police and, most important, the people of Crown Heights could breathe a sigh of relief. All that was left was the finger pointing.

Postmortems

Once peace was restored to Crown Heights and stability replaced the chaos of that violent week, it was time for the Monday morning quarterbacks. Quickly the media and the politicians began dissecting and analyzing what went wrong and, more important in politics, who was to blame.

To the Jewish community, David Dinkins and his administration were to blame inasmuch as the riot had raged out of control for four days. Some of them called it a pogrom, harkening back to the word used to describe the persecution of Jews in Europe since the Middle Ages. The Hasidic community and the New York City Jewish community were outraged that the Lubavitchers were forced to hide inside their houses and apartments as an angry, violent mob howled outside for their blood.

The black community was equally outraged at the extent of the riot, keeping in mind that riots are almost always the works of a criminal element and not representative of the larger community. In this case the American Blacks and the Caribbean Blacks had divergent opinions on the root causes and the activities of those four days.

The black activist community, Daughtry, Sharpton, Maddox, Mason, Moore, Chimurenga and the New York 8, Carson, and a large cast of supporters all pointed to the inequitable treatment of Blacks in Crown Heights to the benefit of the Hasidim. They had been protesting these inequities for years and continuously predicting a "long hot summer." Finally in 1991 they were sadly proven correct. After the riot they were still clamoring for change and accepting no blame for the riot. To some extent they were correct in their assessment of what was wrong in Crown Heights, and they were obviously correct in their prediction of a "long hot summer," if indeed it had not been a self-fulfilling prophecy.

The media naturally was calling for an investigation into what went wrong, and many of the columnists and political pundits were ready to show that they didn't need an investigation to tell them what went wrong. They knew it already. In the *New York Times*, Abe Rosenthal wrote a column detailing the issues, or at least what he thought the issues were. Taking an approach that may be described as Zionist or merely pro-Jewish or perhaps just a realist, his article, entitled Burning the Bridges: The Strategy of the Hate Business, chronicled the "Jew baiting professors on the public payroll" and decrying Wilbert Tatum, the publisher of the Amsterdam News. Rosenthal cut to what he considered the heart of the issue: "Meanwhile these hate hucksters keep pitching anti-Semitism, knowing there would be a special payoff for them in separating Blacks from the particular white community that has given Blacks the most encouragement and the most votes."[8]

In his September 3 column entitled POGROM IN BROOKLYN, Rosenthal pulled no punches and criticized the "hate peddlers," a thinly veiled criticism of the activists who had used Brooklyn as their personal stage. Rosenthal also blamed incompetent, ignorant, or willfully prejudiced journalists as partly to blame for this problem.

Ultimately Rosenthal, a respected American journalist, opined that the events of Crown Heights had greatly undermined the credibility of not only David Dinkins, but sabotaged the electability of other Blacks to the mayor's office.

Rosenthal wasn't wrong in wondering about David Dinkins' viability as a candidate in the upcoming mayoral election. In fact, he was prophetic. Perhaps the biggest beneficiary of the breakdown of the liberal Jewish–Black coalition was the Republican Party, at least in New York, as the election of Rudy Giuliani illustrated. Giuliani's candidacy focused on the problems of the Dinkins administration and particularly on the problems and mistakes of Crown Heights.

Nor was Rosenthal alone in questioning the policies and decisions of Dinkins, especially during the actual riot. He echoed the sentiments and accusations of the Lubavitcher Hasidim and many rank-and-file police officers when he sarcastically asked who was in charge during those violent and lawless days of rioting.[9]

That was certainly a serious charge from a newspaper that had endorsed Dinkins' candidacy in 1989 as he campaigned to become the first African-American mayor of New York City. In the days following the Crown Heights riot, that charge would be raised repeatedly, ultimately (but not quickly) prompting the governor to empanel the commission under Richard Girgenti that would investigate the events of those dramatic days.

It would take Richard Girgenti and his commission two years to finally compile a comprehensive, well written, and accurate chronicle of the riot. It should be noted that the Girgenti Commission report does not categorically place blame in any one direction. While it finds fault in many sectors of the government, not the least of which was an incompetent police response, it also affixes some blame on Deputy Mayor Milton Mollen. But it does not go as far as actually finding serious fault with Mayor Dinkins beyond the usual "buck stops here" mentality, which is tantamount to a public "falling on the sword," what a strong and conscientious leader would do. In that respect it did not seem toharm Dinkins significantly.

In fact, the report seems to be worded ambiguously enough for divergent interpretations. For example, an article by Herb Boyd in the *Amsterdam News* announced that the commission had exonerated the mayor. "The mayor clearly understood his authority to question police officials and to provide them with direction," the report stated. "He exercised this very authority late on Wednesday evening. Mayor Dinkins responded to the report at a Tuesday evening press conference."[10]

The question remained whether that blame would haunt Dinkins. The question was answered in the election of 1993 in which Giuliani unseated Dinkins, the first African-American mayor of New York, leaving after only one term.

The most serious allegations came from the Lubavitcher community and from many other New York Jews: that Mayor Dinkins either gave orders to "let the protestors vent" or he restrained the police officials from doing their job and quelling the disturbance in a timely fashion. This allegation was more than an outcry from the community; it became the integral part of a lawsuit filed against Dinkins, the NYPD, and New York City. Naturally these lawsuits take on a life of their own, and in this case they were ultimately settled out of court by the City.

The Girgenti Commission, created by Executive Order No. 160 by New York State governor Mario Cuomo, began investigating the Crown Heights Riots on November 17, 1992 and released its findings almost a year later in July of 1993. In a highly detailed and fairly thorough investigation of those sordid events, the commission appeared to leave no stone unturned, interviewing 60 members of the NYPD, 40 members of the Crown Heights community, and 15 government officials. Ultimately this commission came up with 36 findings that ran the gamut from analysis of the disturbance itself to assigning blame to Mayor Dinkins for failing to live up to his responsibility for all matters occurring within his jurisdiction and under his watch.

The commission detailed many of the problems and issues that plagued the Crown Heights community in the years leading up to the riots. The commission also found a great number of problems within the NYPD in dealing with the riot, management of manpower, command and control, and overall preparedness for a riot situation such as this one.

But, near the end of the report, finding number 31 states the following: "There is no evidence that Mayor Dinkins, or any City Hall officials, restrained the Police Department from taking aggressive action in response to the disturbance."[11]

The report goes on to acknowledge why that perception existed, citing anecdotal evidence given by cops who said they were told to "hold the line," and by local citizens who observed crimes and beatings happen while cops seemingly stood by and watched. The commission comes close to understanding the problem: While direct orders were given forbidding police officers from taking action on their own without instructions from a supervisor, such a directive, during a civil disorder, is not only standard but prudent."[12]

This analysis appears, on the surface, sound and logical. It appeals to the common sense of the reader, acknowledging the problems that sometimes occur when individual police officers act on their own. The commission continues in that vein:

> However, the utilization of inappropriate tactics, the substitution of ad hoc responses for the implementation of organized plans, and a breakdown in command and control all provide explanations for ineffectual police response. As for a City Hall order, either direct or implicit, no evidence of such was found.[13]

Finally the commission arrived at the crux of the problem. The "ineffectual police response" was not a directive by City Hall, it was the byproduct of micromanagement by City Hall. Not just the City Hall of Mayor Dinkins, but the City Hall of John Lindsay, Abe Beame, Ed Koch, and finally David Dinkins. Beginning with Lindsay's sacking of Police Commissioner Vincent Broderick in 1966[14] for what the mayor deemed a lack of cooperation, City Hall laid claim to the Police Department.[15] Yes, a Police Department that was always clearly and legally under the control of the mayor, but after Lindsay, a Police Department under the sway of politics.

When Mayor Lindsay instructed the cops to go easy on "protests" in underprivileged neighborhoods, the micromanagement of the Police Department became standard operating procedure. When it became apparent to a candidate like Lindsay that his bread was buttered in areas where the police were not well liked, it behooved him to control the damage that a zealous, or perhaps overzealous, force might do to his re-election chances. Whether or not this theory is true, it is cited as gospel throughout the NYPD, as many old-timers cite the Lindsay years as the downfall of not only the Police Department but also New York City.

The veracity of this anecdotal evidence is questionable, but the perception, right or wrong, remains widespread within the department. The politicization of the Police Department became evident in the firings and resignations of high-level police officials that sometimes included the police commissioner himself. Under the moniker of "accountability," this politicization became increasingly prevalent throughout the 80s when this euphemism summed up the prevailing wisdom: "Whatever you do, don't do anything."[16]

From the early days in the Police Academy, recruits were trained to abstain from "independent action," because it could be costly: It could cost you your job. By the mid 1980s the instruction and training in the academy often focused as much on the civil liability ramifications of "independent action" as on the criminal repercussions. Recruits were taught to think about the consequences of everything before taking action. And that was on-duty. If a recruit was off-duty, the order of the day was to refrain at all costs from taking action—call 911! Finally, the recruits were told to leave their guns in their locker. Except when working, the gun could only bring problems for the off-duty cop. Never mind helping to keep the city safe while off-duty. Don't do anything.

Much of this advice was based on that idea of accountability. New York had become a city where the police were no longer respected, but vilified. The characters in the 1981 movie *Fort Apache, The Bronx* epitomized what Hollywood thought was the New York City cop of that era: cynical, corrupt, violent, and essentially, morally bankrupt. In that movie, when the captain of the precinct, the character played by Ed Asner, declares:

"I am here to let the good people of this neighborhood know that there is a thing called the Law and it is going to be enforced," it was as if nobody in the NYPD ever thought of it.

Of course many veterans point to the corruption problems and the methods used to solve those problems as causes of higher crime and increased drug trafficking in the neighborhoods. And to some extent they were right. When uniformed police are forbidden to effect drug arrests and bust crack houses because the potential for corruption is too great, who really suffers? To the honest cops in the NYPD the answer was: the public.

All these issues notwithstanding, there was one incident in the late 1980s that underscored the idea of what political accountability meant in the NYPD, and how one bad decision could ruin a solid if not great career: the Tompkins Square riot of 1988. On that hot, summer night, a group of irate protestors was forced from the park, a historical bastion of protest from an earlier century, by a large contingent of NYPD officers. What happened during the ensuing melee cost that night's duty chief his career. Right or wrong, the perception within the NYPD was that inaction was preferable to action and certainly overreaction.

This perception became a reality for Ray Powers and the Brooklyn South Task Force in 1990 while policing a long-running dispute at a Korean market in the Flatbush section of Brooklyn, the 67th Precinct. What started as a dispute between a Korean store owner and a Haitian customer soon mushroomed into another opportunity for mass protest and the politics of confrontation. The dispute had boiled over and the Korean store owner was arrested. However, the Haitian customer felt that was not enough, and the black activists, Sonny Carson, and his New York 8 were more than happy to take up the fight. So every day a group of protestors gathered in front of the store, shouting and doing their best to discourage customers from entering. It was what came to be called the Korean Boycott. And every day Powers and his Brooklyn South Task Force were out there at Church Avenue and St. Paul's Place keeping the peace.

But the Korean community was not without recourse and soon won an injunction against the protestors. The judge ruled that the protestors could not assemble in front of the store and mandated a boundary line. Initially the NYPD began to enforce this injunction. One day Sonny Carson showed up with a bullhorn and began shouting incendiary and vitriolic rhetoric in front of the store. According to Powers, "I said, 'Sonny, you can't use that bullhorn here.' Carson replied, 'Chief Gallagher allows me to use this in Brooklyn North.' To which Powers retorted, "Sir, Brooklyn North is another country." Powers continued the narrative. "Within five minutes the phone was ringing in the temporary headquarters vehicle. It was the chief of Brooklyn South reaming me out and telling me that he in turn had been reamed out by Chief Scott who, at the time, was the Chief of Patrol."

Within days, the boycotters and protestors were back in front of the store, but word had come down from the Dinkins administration to refer all problems to civil court. Powers recalled, "I then realized that we had taken a criminal matter and made it a civil matter by referring it to civil court. We were disregarding the judge's decision. I realized that we couldn't do anything."

What seemed to evolve was a paralysis of fear within the ranks of the NYPD. From the lowliest rookie emerging from the Police Academy who was trained to eschew taking off-duty action, to the battle-proven duty chief with 30 years of experience, the smart money urged restraint. And often enough, restraint meant doing nothing.

So, when the rocks and bottles started flying on the streets of Crown Heights that hot August evening, it did not require too much imagination to expect that the ranking boss on the scene was urging restraint.

But when the conflagration exploded, it was also not much of a stretch to expect that a 30-year veteran of the NYPD, an Assistant Chief who had seen riots in Harlem in 1964 and in '68 and myriad other incidents, would know exactly what to do and how to handle the disturbance. That is, unless the perception was that this was a potential career-ender. And that is what it was either way for Tom Gallagher, the Assistant Chief and former Borough Commander of Brooklyn North, and for David Dinkins, the former Mayor of New York City.

CHAPTER 10

THE RIOT: AS AMERICAN AS APPLE PIE

The United States of America is a nation spawned from rebellion. One of the first colonial possessions to rise up and vanquish its oppressors, the new Americans declared themselves free to the world and backed up that declaration with patriotic fervor and decisive action. But, as the over-used saying goes: One man's freedom fighter is another man's terrorist. Anything short of victory and George Washington, Sam Adams, Ben Franklin, and the rest of the founding fathers would have found themselves on a gallows instead of dollar bills, monuments, and beer bottles. But the rebellion was successful, in part because of its popularity and also because there was sincere commitment to the cause.

What started as a riot in Boston turned into a revolutionary war. Some of the rioters are now national icons; we celebrate their birthdays and stand in awe of their statues. The dissatisfaction with George III and British arrogance and oppression turned into a freedom fight. The rebellious colonists obviously were fed up and rioted. The riot inspired more action and emboldened additional colonists. Soon it was an uprising and then a Revolutionary War. But it started with dissatisfaction and riot.

In the ensuing years, America was no stranger to voices of discontent and, every so often, riots. Shays' Rebellion and the Whiskey Rebellion were two events that stand out in the early history of this country. And Boston was not the only place given to violent expression and action. The Stamp Act Riot of 1765 is illustrative that colonial New York was also the scene of insurrectionist activity during the early stages of the rebellion against Britain. All of that stopped with the occupation of Manhattan by the Redcoats after the Battle of Long Island. But prior to that fiasco New York was a hotbed of rebellion and, as such, was the scene of patriotic violence.

New York City has always been a stage on which the events of urban life played out. Over the years the city has seen its share of protest, violence, and also riots. Some of those riots predated the Revolutionary War and concerned themselves with other esocial issues, such as the "Negro Riots of 1712."[1] In his compendium, *Great Riots of New York 1712–1873*, T. J. Headley eloquently notes the importance of riots in the historical development of a city:

> The history of the riots that have taken place in a great city from its foundation, is a curious and unique one, and illustrates the peculiar changes in tone and temper that have come over it in the course of its development and growth. They exhibit also one phase of its moral character—furnish a sort of moral history of that vast, ignorant, turbulent class which is one of the distinguishing features of a great city, and at the same time the chief cause of its solicitude and anxiety, and often of dread.[2]

To Headley, the city and the riot are inextricably intertwined. Indeed, the riot is seen as almost a necessity to urban growth. In that respect the riot is an important component of that development. But equally important is how a city reacts to a riot and how a city's leaders respond to the crisis presented by a riot. The response of the New York governor to the Negro Riots of 1712 was certainly decisive, if not ruthless and controversial by today's standards:

> [The Governor] springing from his bed, he rushed out and ordered a cannon to be fired from the ramparts to alarm the town. As the heavy report boomed over the bay and shook the buildings of the town, the inhabitants leaped from their beds and looking out of the windows, saw the sky lurid with flames. Their dread and uncertainty were increased when they heard the heavy splash of soldiers through the mud, and the next moment saw their bayonets gleam out of the gloom, as they hurried forward towards the fire.[3]

Headley's analysis of New York's riots is replete with advice and strategy for fighting these human conflagrations. As hard as it may be to believe, in that era, violence may have been even more commonplace than modern-day New York City. As a result, the response to violent situations, riots, and rebellions was equally if not more violent and deadly. Between 1712 and 1873 Headley lists no fewer than 10 riots, some with colorful names like the Orange Riot, the Flower Riots of 1837, and the Police-Dead Rabbits Riot of 1857. Evidently there was a great deal of unrest in New York City throughout its early history.

During this period, one of the most deadly and infamous riots of New York was the Draft Riots of 1863. Ironically the violent events of that riot prompted the migration of many of Manhattan's black residents across the East River to Brooklyn and the relative safety of a rural area that later came to be called Crown Heights. Many of these people remained in that area, putting down roots. Near the end of the twentieth century Crown Heights would be the scene of its own riot, most likely some of the rioters may have been the descendants of those who fled Manhattan and the anti-Negro violence of 1863.

For America, the early riots were long forgotten. Sadly, very few New Yorkers are aware of the Draft Riots and the events that prompted them. As the Citizens Protective League observed:

> Nations like men are sometimes interested in burying the past. In early 1968 after more than five years marked by political assassinations, racial uprisings, campus disorders, mass demonstrations and the violent suppression of protest, the *New York Times Magazine* asked a group of distinguished scholars to reply to a question, "Is America by nature a violent society?" In answer, University of Chicago anthropologist Clifford Geertz wrote:
>
> "We do not know very well what kind of society we live in, what kind of history we have had, what kind of people we are. We are now just beginning to find out, the hard way"[4]

The 1960s hit America like a ton of bricks. Apparently many of us didn't see it coming. But the causes, the underlying problems, the roots were there all along. The nation simply had its collective head in the sand, ignoring the problems until their weight became unbearable. The result was the calamitous urban riots of 1967 and 1968. These riots brought destruction, violence, death, and suffering. But they also prompted some response. Those riots grabbed America by the shoulders and shook it. The result was an increased awareness of social issues. There was a revolution during those years and we live with the results today. Those awful events were unfortunately another difficult learning process for this country—a necessary evil—but only necessary for a nation that refuses to recognize problems and then find solutions.

The riot might be a necessary evil because it becomes a catalyst for change. It jump-starts the solution process because it grabs the leaders by the head and holds their faces to the unpleasant mess in front of them. Often that unpleasant mess was either created by those leaders or ignorantly allowed to continue as they avoided the ugly and difficult issues. Because elected officials or unelected political hacks refuse to confront the urban problems that make life miserable, they are often confronted with violence in the streets.

Often there is an event, a situation that ignites a combustible situation. In Harlem in 1964 it was the shooting of a black kid by a white police lieutenant. What followed were the Harlem riots, events that posed a stark harbinger of ugly days ahead for New Yorkers. The tone for the rest of the 60s was set. Gone were the innocent Eisenhower years, fading away like an old "Ozzie and Harriet" rerun. Coming onto the screen were street scenes of burning, overturned cars, looting, and violence. Urban America was in flames and the culprits were throwing rocks and bottles in the streets and also watching from the safety of their boardrooms and governmental offices. America was learning some hard lessons in the 60s and experiencing growing pains. Somehow America survived the turbulent 60s and in some ways came away stronger.

But inequities in society remained as social issues continued to divide the country. Urban decay was one of the biggest problems besetting the municipalities as the infrastructure of the large cities crumbled under the weight of increasing populations. Poverty, housing, education, and crime were the central issues of the city and, in the biggest city of all, they were almost always on the front page. Usually, almost exclusively, these were the problems of the black and Hispanic populations. In New York City, a place where the "minority" was quickly becoming the majority, the government was frequently inadequate to the task. Eventually the city would collapse in financial ruin, and the real victims were the poor who were living in the inner city. It was during this period that the early seeds of discontent were sown in the small neighborhood in Brooklyn called Crown Heights.

Ignored or taken for granted by the Democratic political hacks who ruled the city, the Blacks and Hispanics of central Brooklyn were locked in a struggle against poverty and against a city that seemed either incompetent or unwilling to provide assistance. But in Crown Heights these facts of life were exacerbated by additional issues. Crown Heights was one of those true melting pots where many diverse ethnic and racial groups were relegated to living in uncomfortable proximity. Another overused adage is that politics makes for strange bedfellows. In Crown Heights as in New York City, the Democratic Party was the only game in town. So for Crown Heights residents, the battle raged for political patronage and spoils. To the American and Caribbean Blacks it appeared that the recently arrived Lubavitcher Hasidim were reaping these spoils. The result was increasing animosity and heightening tension. But the Democratic Party was in a quandary: How do you keep both sides happy? The answer we have learned is that the Democratic Party ultimately couldn't keep either side happy. And what resulted, along with some additional consequences, was the Crown Heights Riots of 1991.

CHAPTER 11

A HUNGRY MOB IS AN ANGRY MOB

The tension had been building in Crown Heights for more than 30 years. Since the advent of the Maccabees, the black community had resented the efforts and the presence of the Lubavitchers. It only got worse in the 1970s as black people endured occasional assaults at the hands of that group. Of course the other side of the coin was that the Lubavitchers were only trying, in their minds, to make an unsafe neighborhood safer.

The politicians had never taken care of business for various reasons. Clarence Norman Jr. had essentially inherited the Brooklyn Democratic Club leadership, and the Steingut machine was still motoring. No news was good news, as Crown Heights continuously returned Democrats to office. For that reason, not much changed. The housing issues, the school board issues, and any other issues could be alleviatedby money. "Throw money at the problem," was an often-heard criticism of politics in the inner city, but if the accusation was true, then the real losers were the poor people. Not the poor of spirit, or not even the poor of money. The people who suffered were poor from lack of political clout. And Herbert Daughtry recognized it back in 1977 when Community Board #9 was created.

On our weekly Sunday morning WWRL radio the following week, I preached a sermon entitled "The Agony of Powerlessness." I analyzed our situation and attempted to show that the powerless will always get a "raw deal." I urged unity and the development of political and economic power, my continuing theme. I criticized the Hasidim for their misuse of power, and also criticized our Black leaders for not organizing our people to exercise power for our own interests:

Let us suppose the Hasidic Jews had tried to ingratiate themselves or, shall I say, tried to Uncle Goldstein their way to power. Do you think anything would have been gained? Probably here and there somebody would have felt sorry for them and given them a few jobs and some poverty bucks, but nothing really substantial.

However, by organizing themselves first, then making demands, they made success depend upon their own strength.[2]

That may have been the start of the serious unrest. Daughtry became energized in a different way from the New York 8, but in his own way he recognized the issues and confronted them. By the 1990s he was joined by that crew (the New York 8) of demonstrators and Sharpton's group of activists also. They may not have been looking for a spark, but it came nonetheless.

The Motorcade

On Monday night, August 19, 1991 Josef Lifsh was driving the last car of the rebbe's motorcade. That day they had visited the graves of the rebbe's in-laws; his father-in-law was his predecessor as grand rebbe of the Lubavitcher Court of Hasidim. At about 8:20 p.m. the motorcade returned on the usual route and made a left off of Eastern Parkway onto Rochester Avenue and then a right on President Street. Some witnesses stated that the motorcade was traveling pretty fast. Lifsch was trying to keep up. There was a 71st Precinct cruiser leading the motorcade. As Lifsch approached the corner of Utica Avenue, the light, according to witnesses, had been changing. Lifsch continued through the intersection, collided with a van that had been driving north-bound on Utica and then Lifsch's car careened onto the sidewalk on President Street.[3]

Gavin Cato and his cousin Angela had been riding their bikes on the sidewalk when Josef Lifsch changed their world forever. Gavin's world ended as he was crushed between the bumper of the car and the wall of the building. Angela miraculously survived. At the time, every effort, despite claims to the contrary, were made to save them.[4]

Almost immediately a 71st Precinct car showed up on the scene and Police Officer Nona Capace surveyed the scene. She recognized a potential riot. Unintentionally and unfortunately, her actions only may have exacerbated things. When the ambulances showed up, one from Hatzolah the Hasidic ambulance and other manned by NYC EMS workers, she told the Hatzolah driver to take Josef Lifsch away from the scene. Already the crowd had been trying to hurt him, and they might have had it not been for some level-headed local black men who interceded on his behalf. Meanwhile the EMS workers were working valiantly on Gavin Cato, an eight-year-old boy fighting for his life. He was hopelessly mangled and would be pronounced dead at nearby Kings County Hospital. Angela Cato had a better chance and she was removed by another ambulance. She survived the horrible accident. But the neighborhood almost did not.

Within minutes of the accident, even while the victims and the driver were still present on the scene, people began yelling, inciting a gathering crowd. This was a melting pot neighborhood that did not need a lot of stirring. The issues were already more than close to the surface. The Cato cousins were of Trinidadian descent and the neighborhood knew them. As a result, the crowd that formed at the scene of the accident soon turned violent and branched out through the neighborhood, causing havoc.

B.B. King, the blues guitarist and legend, had been giving a concert in nearby Wingate High School field and a detail of NYPD cops had been assigned there.[5] Captain Vincent Kennedy was completing his first day as the commanding officer of the 71st Precinct. The concert had been going on peacefully until Kennedy learned of the accident and the resulting violence on President Street. He immediately sent approximately 35 officers of his Wingate detail up to the scene of the accident. Normally his actions would have been sufficient, but on this night, the crowd had already mobilized and was no longer congregated at the original scene.

Rampaging mobs of black youths stormed through the streets of Crown Heights, yelling ethnic and anti-Semitic slurs, sometimes attacking Hasidic men and women they happened on. One of these victims, Liev Spielman, was saved by a local black man as he was beset by an angry mob at the accident scene. While the crowd surrounded him, this black man grabbed Spielman and yelled to the crowd, "He's mine and I'm going to have him arrested." Spielman recounted that the man led him away from the crowd to a safer area and then told Spielman that he owed him one.[6]

Yankel Rosenbaum was not as lucky. A visiting Talmudic scholar from Australia, Rosenbaum had been returning to his Crown Heights residence from a day of studies. But the streets on his usual route were now filled with danger. Unaware of the peril, Rosenbaum was jumped by a group of 10 to 15 black youths who reportedly yelled anti-Semitic remarks as they attacked. One of the youths repeatedly stabbed Rosenbaum who fell to the ground, mortally wounded. The mob fled as the police arrived, but Lemrick Nelson, a black Trinidadian teen was apprehended near the scene.[7] A bloody knife was found inside his pocket. He was brought back to the scene of the stabbing and was identified by Rosenbaum, who asked Nelson why he had done it.

Rosenbaum was removed to Kings County Hospital, where the Cato cousins had been taken. Although his wounds should not have been life-threatening, Rosenbaum died of internal bleeding. Apparently the doctors had not been aware of all his stab wounds. Gavin Cato was a victim of the accident and had already died. Yankel Rosenbaum was the first victim of the riot. This incident would take on a life of its own long after the flames of the riot had died down. In what would become a torturous and lengthy legal proceeding, the entire Crown Heights neighborhood would endure three trials and the ultimate conviction of Nelson for manslaughter. In what can only be described as an American legal travesty, it would take almost 13 years for this crime to be adjudicated as Nelson pled guilty in federal court to stabbing Rosenbaum. By that time he had spent close to 10 years in prison.

All day the streets of Crown Heights grew increasingly dangerous, especially for Jews, but in reality for anyone. The angry mobs were marching up and down President Street, Utica Avenue, and other blocks. Stores were burning, cars were overturned, and windows were smashed. There was some looting and the police response itself was disturbing. But by 4:00 a.m. the angry mobs had dissipated and an eerie calm returned to the streets.[8] This would not be the most violent night of the riot, but it was the only night that a death had directly resulted from the violence, so in one respect it might be described as the most deadly night of the Crown Heights riot.

"Two Underdogs Colliding"[9]

The radical events of Monday night ended early on Tuesday morning. It was during this period that the NYPD apparently let things slip out of control. Although Tuesday morning was relatively tranquil, by midafternoon the situation had once again become agitated and tense. Demonstrators returned to the streets of Crown Heights but significantly, there had not been a major influx of police reserves. What retired Chief Ray Powers had described as an "ineffectual mobilization" took place in the vicinity of the accident scene. A mobilization is the method by which the police assemble a detail of officers to police an event, a demonstration, or a riot. There are various levels of mobilizations depending on the criticality of the circumstances. In this instance, the prevailing wisdom suggests that the NYPD did not accurately assess the situation and, consequently, the response was insufficient and lacking. This led to increased violence by the mob that recognized their advantage in sheer numbers.

"We could have wrapped this thing up on Monday night, but there was no game plan," said a detective in the 71st Precinct on Empire Boulevard in Crown Heights."[10] This criticism of the NYPD response reported by the *New York Times* underscored an even more significant assessment of the police by acting Chief of Patrol Mario Selvaggi, who was the senior official in charge at Crown Heights: "We saw then and there that we had to adjust and change our tactics."[11]

But the NYPD took two days to make those adjustments. To many it seemed that there had been a vacuum of leadership, and the result was chaos in the streets. The observation by the *New York Times* was a situation where there was "aggression by one group against another; two underdogs colliding."[12] But a lot of criticism was directed toward the police in the streets, the rank and file who were standing there, separating the Hasidim and the black community, feeling the wrath of both groups. The Hasidim were angry because they felt they weren't being protected, their constitutional rights were being denied. Many of them felt that they had become prisoners in their own homes.[13] The word pogrom was being used, in the streets and in the media, as the journalists each put their own spin on the situation.[14] Whatever the spin might be there was no denying the violence and the chaos in the streets.

Interviewed for this project, Timothy Horner is a retired captain from the NYPD. At the time of the Crown Heights Riots he was a lieutenant in the Brooklyn North Task Force, which performed the same job as the Brooklyn South Task Force, policing demonstrations and doing riot control. During the Crown Heights riot each borough's task force was initially mobilized to the area, and Horner was present on the first night and each succeeding night of the riot.

"There is no doubt that the entire event that night [Monday night] was mismanaged. Certainly management dropped the ball—there was no coordination. No one took charge, there was no one who took responsibility or command.

"But one thing did impress me and that was the cops. The cops, for the most part, were professional. They took care of business and they did it professionally. They knew what to do. But they needed someone to take command."

"Things did not change for almost three days. There seemed to be no coordination. Although there were some chiefs present at the scene, none of them seemed to take overall command. Part of the reason was that this riot was taking place on the border of two NYPD Patrol Boroughs. Eastern Parkway was the dividing line between Brooklyn North and Brooklyn South, and the rioters and kids would be running back and forth between the two Patrol Boroughs. It was difficult to get a handle on that."

"Nobody wanted to get in the middle of it. Everybody seemed to be waiting for the Mayor to make a call. So for three days things were out of control. Finally on the third day the word came down to make arrests; to enforce the law. Then everything changed. More reinforcements showed up and finally we had enough manpower to take care of things. Previously we had been merely trying to control the crowd. Essentially, nobody took charge."

"NO ONE ASKED ME"

– FIRST DEPUTY COMMISSIONER RAYMOND KELLY ON WINS

The vacuum of leadership at the top of the NYPD had been created by a confluence of unrelated circumstances. Chief of Department Robert J. Johnston had ruled the NYPD for the better part of eight years. He was a firm and commanding presence in the Department. He had formerly been the Commanding Officer of Brooklyn South, and some said that he owed his promotion to Chief of Department to political influence from the Hasidim in the 71st and the 66th precincts. But Johnston had retired after more than 35 years in the NYPD. His last day had been August 16, 1991. His successor was Chief David Scott, the former Chief of Patrol who had commanded the Brooklyn Bridge fiasco in 1989. Now Scott was promoted to Chief of Department, but he had taken vacation. The acting chief had been Joseph Borelli, normally the Chief of Detectives. Chief Mario Selvaggi had been promoted to Chief of Patrol on the day the riot started. It was a literally baptism by fire.

At the apex of this whole command structure was the Police Commissioner, Lee P. Brown, who had been appointed by Mayor Dinkins following his inauguration a year earlier. But Lee Brown's nickname had followed him from Houston where he had also been police commissioner. He was called "Out of Town Brown," an inference that he was frequently out of town when his presence was needed locally. There is no evidence that Brown was indeed out of town when the Crown Height riot began. He met with Mayor Dinkins at Kings County Hospital early on Tuesday morning.

The second highest ranking police official in the NYPD is the First Deputy Police Commissioner. Lee Brown had appointed Assistant Chief Raymond Kelly as his First Deputy. Kelly was perhaps the most qualified person for the job, if not the Commissioner's job.[15] Kelly had worked his way up through the ranks of the NYPD after retiring from active duty in the United States Marine Corps. He was still a colonel in the

Reserves and would actually see duty in the Gulf War of 1991. Kelly also held a Master's degree from Harvard and was a graduate of local Manhattan College. Beyond his academic and military qualifications, Kelly had been a cop in Brooklyn and was formerly the commanding officer of the 71st Precinct. He had the respect of the men and women in the NYPD and the respect of the community. He had the reputation of being a no-nonsense man with common sense and compassion.

For this reason, everyone expected Ray Kelly to step in and take charge. But the NYPD was a funny organization. Kelly was no longer a uniform commander, and the uniform commanders took charge when riots happened. At least that's the way it would have been if Robert Johnston had still been Chief of Department. Regardless, Kelly was not a visible presence on the scene until late Tuesday afternoon, which may have been the most violent day of the riot. When asked why he had not taken charge earlier, Kelly responded, "No one asked me."

But it is Ray Kelly who has been credited with stepping in and restoring order to the situation. The events of Wednesday, particularly the inability of Mayor Dinkins to speak to the crowd and the perilous situation he encountered when he tried to convene a press conference at P.S. 167 may have been the impetus needed to change the police tactics. Deputy Mayor Bill Lynch himself had described a chaotic and threatening situation as he arrived on the scene prior to the mayor. Apparently these developments served as a wake-up call to the mayor, and may have formed the impetus for action.

> To me police [were] everywhere. I'm wondering what's happening and what has happened is a group of kids had come running, threw rocks, bottles at reporters that were at the school and they wouldn't let the Mayor through. That's ... That concerned me deeply. I ... They held the Mayor up ... I had now, you know, seen this thing. It's Wednesday that gets me really in focus.[16]

Another deputy mayor also seemed to find some focus after a bottle crashed between him and the mayor. Deputy Mayor Milton Mollen had accompanied the mayor to the Cato residence on President Street. He found the situation extremely dangerous:

> The Mayor and I got out of the car and we started to walk with bodyguards—the Mayor's bodyguards, I don't have any bodyguards—to the building ... as they were walking ... to the building, we walked probably a distance of approximately fifty feet or thereabouts. There were bottles being hurled. One went right through. I was walking right alongside the Mayor, [and] one went right between us.[17]

Those events seemed to put everything in perspective. If the mayor himself and his deputies weren't safe, then who was? Certainly not the police who were getting hurt in increasing numbers. Certainly the Hasidim themselves did not feel safe, and as crime statistics showed, the violence was spreading into the nearby 77th Precinct where innocent bystanders, non-Jews, were being assaulted. Even the media was not safe as Jimmy Breslin found out on Utica Avenue. The livery cab transporting him to the area was stopped in traffic and he was pulled from the vehicle and attacked. Soon, reports of a naked white man running for his life were being circulated. It only brought a smile to the cops' faces when they learned that a chagrined but relatively unharmed Breslin had sought safety in the 77th Precinct station house. The mob had stolen his pants.

By Thursday morning, First Deputy Commissioner Kelly had devised a new, proactive plan for quelling the riot. The police would abandon the "fixed-post" strategy that had been employed in the early days. Kelly divided the riot area into sectors, saturated with foot patrols and supplemented by roving, mobile response units that would be able to apprehend groups causing trouble and committing crimes. Arrests would now be in order.

Although Thursday was a violent day, it also marked the turning point in the riot. The police arrested 61 people on Thursday night, more than all of the other three days combined.[18] By Friday, relative calm had returned to Crown Heights. The new tactics of the NYPD, the proactive approach, and the arrests all were effective. But perhaps the most effective measure was the display by the police that they would no longer brook any nonsense. On Thursday the police demonstrated that the rule of law was once again in effect, and the rioters seemed to understand this. By Friday night, Crown Heights was an armed camp with an undercurrent of tension. Like a war-ravaged city now occupied by a conquering army, Crown Heights now had to pick up the pieces and repair the cracks in the melting pot.

The Girgenti Report

Of all the pieces that had to be picked up, the community of course was the most important one, but there were indications that the situation was not as hopeless as the riot indicated. Many in the Crown Heights Community, many of the Caribbean Blacks, some of the American Blacks, and even some in the Hasidic community felt that many of the rioters were not from the immediate community. There certainly had been many outside agitators, and although there would never be conclusive evidence, it appeared that much of the violence was the work of young criminals with an axe to grind, not the product of community residents.

One local politician who supported that idea was Mary Pinkett, a longtime Crown Heights community activist and elected community board member:

There are people using this tragic accident for their own political purposes. I saw the marchers in the street and didn't recognize anyone. As I rode through the neighborhood, the community people were sitting in front of their houses. They wanted their children home. They were not milling around in crowds waiting for something to happen."[19]

Retired Chief Ray Powers and other members of the Brooklyn South Task Force agreed that the local neighborhood people were actually supportive of the police, oftentimes providing the beleaguered cops with soda and water. According to Powers, this was a frequent sight on President Street during the afternoons and evenings, even during the heaviest periods of rioting.

Mary Pinkett had long been at odds with others in the black community and some of this is evident as she recounts the issues leading up to the riot:

The incident was a culmination of anger. The complaint the blacks have is the racism of American society. When you bring that conflict together with the situation that happened the other night—a child is killed and another is critically injured and an ambulance arrives and the crowd is menacing the occupants of the ambulance and then the police tell the ambulance to go ("take your people and go") without evaluating the injured youngsters—to the crowd it says that they did not care about the children. They did not care about us. With this in mind all the anger is taken out on the ambulance drivers. There were those who were trying to make it into a deliberate act against us. I don't believe it was deliberate. If a pattern of preference was already there and a situation occurs, that people can see it they say, "See this is what I have been telling you all along."[20]

Retired Detective Bill Crowe was working in Brooklyn South Homicide and was present at the hospital when Gavin Cato died, and when Yankel Rosenbaum arrived and later died. Crowe was interviewed for this project and came to a conclusion similar to Pinkett's:

One simple act might have avoided all that bloodshed and violence. If the Hatzollah ambulance had just taken the injured kids to KCH [Kings County Hospital] it would have most likely diffused the situation. It would have been a tremendous show of good will and it would probably have saved Yankel Rosenbaum's life. There might not have been a riot.

What Crowe could not have known, because he wasn't at the chaotic scene, was that Gavin Cato and his cousin Angela were already being treated by City EMS workers as the Hatzolah pulled away with Josef Lifsch, the driver of the vehicle. But Crowe's sentiments underscore the history of racial and ethnic relations in the neighborhood, a situation that was implicitly understood in the immediate community. The perception was often the reality, and on the night of August 19, that perception started a riot.

The aftermath of any controversial and critical incident inevitably leads to the politics of finger-pointing; the Monday-morning quarterbacking. Naturally an event as important and tragic as Crown Heights, or any riot for that matter, becomes political fodder for the pundits, journalists, and elected officials. This was immediately the case in Crown Heights. *The New York Times* issued a stern rebuke of the mayor and the Police Department and *Times* correspondents called the riot a "pogrom."[21] The *Amsterdam News* was critical of Dinkins for different reasons, citing the non-arrest of Lifsch for reckless driving. *The Jewish Daily Forward* also called it a pogrom. The Hasidic community and the Rosenbaum family immediately initiated a lawsuit against the city and other defendants. There was plenty of vitriol to go around.

For all of the recriminations and blame assignments, it is interesting to note that it took almost two years before a government report on the riot was issued. It took that long because it was a full year before Governor Mario Cuomo issued Executive Order No. 160, which called for the empaneling of an investigative commission. Curiously enough the report was released in July of 1993, approximately three months prior to the New York City mayoral election. The committee was chaired by Richard Girgenti, the director of Criminal Justice Services for New York State. As a result the Commission's report was called "A Report to the Governor on the Disturbances in Crown Heights: An Assessment of the City's Preparedness to Civil Disorder." Almost everyone in New York referred to it as the Girgenti Report.

In his introductory letter to the governor, Girgenti purports to have conducted an "exhaustive analysis to document what occurred during the most extensive racial unrest New York City has experienced in over twenty years." With a large investigative staff (8 investigators), 18 analysts and writers, and what appears to be a blue ribbon panel of team leaders replete with three Ph.D.s, the "Commission Report" on the surface was an extensive and fairly comprehensive report. It was intelligently written and told the story in a straightforward, readable manner. But the report, for all its pages and interviews failed to get to the crux of the issue; it failed to assign conclusive blame in any large dosage.

The commission blamed the Police Department extensively, citing lack of preparation and lack of training, and significantly faulted the field commander for choosing "a restraint-oriented approach, but failed to direct proactive measures to end the violence." Interviews for this report with subordinate commanders such as Lieutenant Horner and Captain Powers support that theory. But Powers' own recollection was that Chief Thomas Gallagher, the Field Commander on the first two nights, did indeed know what to do. The inference was that the lack of proactive policing was not a result of Gallagher's indecision or ineptitude. It was an entrenched philosophy of the Police Department since the 1960s and it only got worse in the 1990s following the Tompkins Square Riot in 1988.

But the commission did not solely blame the NYPD, although that organization received a significant amount of the blame, including Finding No. 15: "A collective failure by top-ranking NYPD officials delayed the implementation of appropriate tactics to control this Disorder."[22] This finding almost bears out the underlying nature of the NYPD leadership. To take action in the NYPD was sometimes tantamount to political or professional suicide.

The last finding by the commission finds fault with Mayor Dinkins' response to the disturbance, but in reality was a mere political slap on the wrist: "Finding 36: The Mayor, as the City's Chief Executive, did not act in a timely and decisive manner in requiring the Police Department to meet his own stated objectives: 'to protect the lives, safety and property of the residents of Crown Heights, and to quickly restore peace and order to the community.'"[23]

This criticism of the mayor falls into the category of "the buck stops here," yet fails to address the issue that roiled the passions of New York City. That issue was the claim by Hasidim and others that the Police Department deliberately held back and allowed the rioting to occur for a significant period of time. In fact, that claim was at the heart of a lawsuit filed by Hasidim and the Rosenbaum family against Mayor Dinkins and New York City.

In Finding 31, the Girgenti Commission absolved the mayor and his staff: There is no evidence that Mayor Dinkins, or any city hall officials, restrained the Police Department from taking aggressive action in response to the disturbance."[24] In the body of that finding the commission asserts that no one was able to prove those allegations and that any order given on the street that restrained police officers from independent action was "not only standard but prudent." In effect it was an indirect absolution for City Hall and another knock on the police commanders. A legitimate question must be posed here: Why were there so few arrests the first days of the riot, when the police knew that arresting agitators would decrease the propensity for violence? Why wouldn't a police commander order his troops to make arrests?

The Girgenti Commission blamed Mayor Dinkins in a generic way; he was the mayor so anything that happens under his watch was his fault. But the commission didn't castigate Dinkins nor did it indicate that the conditions that preceded the riot were his fault. As New York City politics have shown us, many of those conditions were not of his creation.

David Dinkins

Mayor David N. Dinkins was the 106th mayor, the first African-American mayor of New York City. He had been a long-time player in the New York City Democratic machine, a clubhouse politician who had been the Manhattan Borough president and also the New York City clerk. In some respect Dinkins was proof that loyalty to the party and perseverance could lead to great political success. His mayoralty had been heralded as a time of healing for the city, as many black residents were looking forward to some long-desired political clout. But Dinkins encountered problems that were not of his creation, problems that had been festering for years under previous Democratic administrations. Many in the city, especially Herbert Daughtry, looked at the 12-year Koch regime as a time of great divisiveness on racial and ethnic lines. Everybody was hoping that Dinkins would be able to change that.

The Korean boycott situation was the early harbinger of problems for Dinkins and New York City. Politics of confrontation was a fact of life in Brooklyn as the Revs. Daughtry and Sharpton proved on a regular basis. The presence of Sonny Carson and the New York 8 was another incendiary ingredient added to the combustible recipe. Many police officials point to the Korean boycott as the precursor to Crown Heights because it indicated that Dinkins and, as an extension, the New York City Police Department, were not willing or able to enforce the law. Some in the city viewed this situation as more stirring of the proverbial pot. Whatever the reality, Dinkins' response to the situation has been criticized from all sides and did nothing to burnish his reputation as a healer or conciliator.

David Dinkins had the final word in the Girgenti Commission Report, which was fitting. If the intention of the report was to find fault or assign blame to the mayor, then it seems only fair that he should get a chance to defend his actions or the appearance of lack of action. Over 19 pages Dinkins detailed, in chronological order, the events of that violent, dramatic week. He also explained the efforts he made and the effect they had on the events that were swirling in the streets of Crown Heights. His statement is in every way a defense or perhaps a justification of his administration and the method by which it handled a tense and difficult situation. There is little explanation of events and issues of the past that were part of the build-up to this riot, although he acknowledged being aware of the disparities, perceived or real, within the community when he addressed a press conference on Tuesday, August 20, 1991:

> Further, I reported that the Cato children received immediate medical treatment from the City emergency medical technicians who arrived at the scene simultaneously with the Hatzolah ambulance. I addressed the perception by some in the African-American Community that the Hasidic community consistently received preferential treatment by the police.[25]

His report also detailed the frustrating problems of dealing with the purveyors of the politics of confrontation; the Revs. Daughtry and Sharpton, attorneys Maddox and Moore, and the Sonny Carson contingent. Dinkins made it clear that this group of activists made the situation more difficult, the inflammatory rhetoric and angry protest marches during those tense days were not helpful to a mayor trying to negotiate a peaceful conclusion to a violent and potentially deadly situation. His frustration is apparent as his negotiations with this group were unsuccessful; an African-American mayor trying to do his job and protect life and property while understanding and maybe empathizing with the issues raised by these activists. It was the paradox of his mayoralty. Part of his own constituency was causing problems during the most critical event of his tenure.

The mayor also acknowledged ultimate responsibility for the mismanagement of the situation by the NYPD. He admitted that his primary objectives set forth on page 3, to "protect the lives, safety, and property of the residents of Crown Heights, and to quickly restore peace and order to the community" were not met in a timely fashion. He strongly disputed the "unfounded allegations concerning the actions of City Hall officials, either First Deputy Mayor Norman Steisel, nor Deputy Mayor Milton Mollen, nor Deputy Mayor Bill Lynch, nor I, nor any other official at City Hall ever gave any direction, either express or implied, that the police department should hold back in any manner whatsoever during this period of time." Dinkins maintained that those allegations were completely untrue. There is no evidence to suggest they were true beyond the doubts expressed by observers that all those police commanders with so many years of experience could not know how to quell a disturbance and by incompetence allow it to degenerate into a full-blown riot.

Mayor Dinkins concluded by stating that "the police mis-perceived that their initial tactical response could quickly end the violence ... On Wednesday night August 22, 1991, it was clear that the police response was not effective in controlling the disturbance. This led to my late night meeting with the Police Commissioner at Kings County Hospital, where I questioned the effectiveness of the police tactics and emphasized that further steps needed to be considered."[26]

Those conclusions, coupled with the findings by the Commission effectively placed the blame for the events on the police and, by extension, the mayor. The mayor acknowledged that, as the leader of the city, he must accept ultimate blame. Almost in the same breath he claimed credit for turning the event around by forcing the police department to see the error of its ways. In the end the mayor was both noble in accepting blame and heroic in forcing the police to do their job.

A Separate Peace?

Following the events of the Crown Heights Riot in 1991, a scarred community was forced to come to grips with reality; neither of the two groups at odds with each other was going to leave town. They were stuck with each other. And it must be said that almost immediately efforts were under way to heal the community. One significant development was the commitment by Hasidic leaders to march in the impending Labor Day Carnival parade. They marched, and things were peaceful. There were a lot of crossed fingers on both sides of the street. Another development has been chronicled in a film that follows the escapades of a multi-ethnic/racial basketball team from Crown Heights. It is a hopeful film that acknowledges problems while extolling the healing process that is taking place. One of the heroes of this effort was also one of the heroes of the riots, Richard Green. A community board official, Green was hailed by both sides as a conciliator, a man who cared deeply about the community and puts his words into action through community outreach programs.

Through the years following the riot, the trials of Lemrick Nelson, the law suit filed by the Rosenbaum family and the vitriolic verbiage of the 1993 mayoral election, Crown Heights endured as a community somewhat divided by race and ethnicity but united in a commitment to live together and to make it work. It is a work in progress, a project that can show America that the Melting Pot is real and viable. Although the accident and resulting riot were flashpoints that made that Melting Pot boil over, there is evidence that the Melting Pot is still intact.

CHAPTER 12

THE MEDIA RETURNS A VERDICT

In the aftermath of the Crown Heights Riots of 1991, political and social commentators weighed in from all sides. On the media side there were observations and critiques from the divergent camps. On the streets the battle had subsided, but the dust had barely cleared and the media was pointing fingers and laying blame. In the *New York Times* various commentators and reporters wrote about the culture of black anti-Semitism that had evolved in the community. The *Amsterdam News* leveled criticism at David Dinkins and the Hasidic community, pointing out that the riot was the product of years of social inequities in that neighborhood and in New York City.

Reporters in the *New York Times* described the fallout from the violent events, the funeral of Gavin Cato, and the vitriolic and, at times, incendiary political rhetoric emanating from Revs. Sharpton and Daughtry. In the words of Daughtry: "The violence that followed Gavin's death was only a lick of the fire next time."[1] Sharpton's commentary was equally dramatic when he "linked Cato with the four young black girls killed in Birmingham, Alabama." He described the incident, "Not a mere car accident but rather 'the social accident of apartheid.'"[2]

A few days earlier Ari Goldman in the *New York Times* described "The cauldron of hate that kept bubbling and by week's end there were two dead." Goldman's account included a Hasidic commentary: "We have managed to restrain our community for the last four days, and that has not been easy."[3]

But the basic reporting contemporary to the events did little to shed light on what many people on either side felt were the root causes of the riot. It would take some time for the dust to clear and the real acrimony to rise to the surface. In the interim much has been written about this event, but two authors seem to have captured the opposing viewpoints. In the January 1993 edition of *The Jewish Daily Forward*, Philip Gourevitch went to great lengths to detail the dynamic at work in Crown Heights and New York City before, during, and after the riot.

In the article "The Crown Heights Riot and Its Aftermath," Gourevitch pulled no punches when he blamed the rising "Black Anti-Semitism" of the intellectual black community. Blaming the "demagogues" who he felt fanned the flames of this anti-Semitism, Gourevitch cited the racial double standard that existed not only in New York City but in America, as well. In somewhat muted terms he blamed David Dinkins and his preference for the Blacks and complained about what he terms "the false paradigm of black victimization." But Gourevitch acknowledged that Dinkins was not intentionally biased in this incident, rather it was an error of myopia.

Gourevitch made it clear who is to blame, once again blaming the "demagogues" who fanned the flames and the prevalent racism and anti-Semitism:

> Most importantly, it was a riot not by victims of racism but by racists, an attack on Jews because they were Jews. Blacks shouting anti-Semitic slogans, and explicitly proclaiming themselves the proud reincarnations of Hitler, sought to destroy and/or drive out their Jewish neighbors by force.[4]

Finally Gourevitch addressed one of the key complaints from the Jewish community; that Dinkins intentionally allowed the riot to rage for a couple of days. Falling in line with almost every other analysis of this event, Gourevitch acknowledged that this was not the case, although certainly it had been established that mistakes were made both by the police and by City Hall. Concluding his comments, Gourevitch underscored the idea of the double standard in New York City politics, wondering whether Mayor Dinkins would address the problems presented by the "racism, the anti-Semitism, and the lawlessness that were so frighteningly manifested in Crown Heights and that were then tolerated and for too long justified by the mindless application of a false paradigm of black victimization." Gourevitch was clear in his criticism that David Dinkins was slow in condemning black violence in Crown Heights and, therefore, was part of the problem before he became part of the solution.

Perhaps the most dramatic and unapologetic literature came from one of the central figures of the event, Rev. Herbert Daugtry. *No Monopoly on Suffering* was Daughtry's personal account of the lead-up to Crown Heights and a defense of his role in the events. It provides both historical commentary and political invective, as Daughtry leaves no stone unturned and then picks up some of those stones and hurls them. In this book, the chapter entitled "The Politics of Confrontation" quote Daughtry extensively, perhaps violating a long-standing aversion to lengthy quotes, in an effort to allow one of the main actors to tell his story. How many people have read *No Monopoly on Suffering*[5] or his other work on this subject, *Inside the Storm*?[6]

In those works Daughtry painstakingly itemized the problems and the inequities he felt were put on the black community of Crown Heights by the New York City government by virtue of the Hasidic political influence. His books are litanies of all the injustices and problems of life in Brooklyn. While Daughtry took great pains to describe the building tension and the events leading up to the riot in Crown Heights, he also pointedly addressed the issues brought up by the Jewish press, black anti-Semitism:

> Isn't it ironic that I and other Black leaders, who have known unparalleled oppression at the hands of practically everybody, be charged with anti-Semitism? It calls to mind what Malcolm X used to say when he was accused of being racist: "Here we have a knife in our back, and when we scream, twist, and turn to get the knife out of our back, we are called anti-Semitic or racist." Black people in America do not have a history of discrimination against any people. However, we do have a history of struggling against those who oppress and exploit us. Whoever they may be.[7]

Two descriptions of an event, two literary works seeking to analyze and assess the situation, both finding blame on the other side while barely addressing their own culpability. Maybe the *New York Times* said it best when it described the Crown Heights Riots as "Two underdogs colliding."

Both groups were intent on carving their own niche and grabbing their own piece of the American Dream. Both groups have come from another world where they were oppressed and persecuted, and both groups have experienced similar treatment on these shores. They find themselves living side-by-side, at times in acrimony but both looking for harmony. Perhaps Daughtry's title aptly describes the situation for both groups: *No Monopoly on Suffering.*

CHAPTER 13 POLICING IN NEW YORK CITY: THE HANDCUFFS COME OFF

The streets were quiet, the fires had gone out, and the neighborhood was crowded with uniform police officers. Crown Heights had become an armed camp. The NYPD had reverted to its usual policy of manpower overkill. The common practice at special events, referred to as a "detail" in NYPD jargon, was to make sure there were more than enough officers assigned. No matter what neighborhood, there would be a plethora of officers at the detail. An overwhelming show of force almost always discouraged would-be trouble makers from perpetrating any criminal activity.

By Friday the NYPD had brought the situation under control and, with order, restored the neighborhood calm, but with nervous undertones. With four or five cops on each corner it would be surprising to encounter any more trouble. Now it was NYPD business as usual. The question posed by many was: Why had it taken three days to implement this approach?

The answers were unclear as an embarrassed NYPD tried to figure out what had gone wrong. To many of the rank and file and the lower-level supervisors, the answer was obvious and it harkened back to the riot at the Brooklyn Bridge: There were not enough cops on hand to quell the rioters. And the high-ranking supervisors on the scene did not empower those cops to take proper police action to stop the violent actions of the mob. The cops from the Brooklyn South Task Force said this in the aftermath of the Brooklyn Bridge Riot and they repeated the assertion after Crown Heights. Cops, especially task force cops, knew what to do in these riot situations, but they were well trained to wait for instructions from the field commanders. This is where the situation becomes complicated and murky.

A Hands-Off Policy

"The New York City Police Department is still largely a political institution, deeply rooted in the same machine politics that has dominated New York for a century."[1]

–Sindney L. Haring and Gerda W. Ray

Since the days of Mayor Lindsay, the job of police commissioner had become more politicized. When Lindsay sacked commissioner Vincent Broderick in 1966, citing the commissioner's independence and his opposition to the proposed Civilian Complaint Review Board, the mayor set the tone for future commissioners and mayors. In the minds of many political observers at the time, Lindsay had made a politically calculated decision in firing Broderick. Lindsay was advocating a more hands-off policy on the streets.[2] The mayor favored the Review Board for a variety of reasons, one of them being that it appealed to the minority community of New York. Lindsay wanted civilian oversight of the NYPD and Broderick retorted that there already was civilian oversight. So Broderick walked. Many of the cops felt that Lindsay had taken the side of the perpetrators and had undermined the credibility of the police. In their mind, Lindsay had made it more difficult for the police to keep the city safe.[3]

Not coincidentally, crime began to rise significantly in New York City. Soon the moniker "Fun City" was being used derisively by the media. Central Park became a dangerous place as crime shot through the roof. The fiscal problems that plagued New York City in the late 60s and into the mid 70s only exacerbated the problem. Police layoffs, hiring freezes, and attrition additionally robbed the NYPD of its ability to police the city. But another dynamic was also at work.

The precedent set by Lindsay, the politicization of the police commissioner's office, had far-reaching effects in the NYPD. The cops felt that the so-called hands-off policies had effectively handcuffed them. Many observers felt that the criminals had secured the upper hand as crime spiraled out of control. To complicate matters, the late 1960s also saw a rise in police corruption. It seems that about every twenty years New York City endures a period of police corruption that culminates in the appointment of a blue ribbon commission tasked with eradicating the problem.[4]

The Knapp Commission

Tales of corruption had been increasing through the late 1960s as morale in the NYPD was sagging. The final straw was the release of the book *Serpico*, the biographical story of plainclothes detective Frank Serpico and his seemingly one-man crusade to battle the endemic and systemic corruption thriving in the NYPD.[5] When in 1973 Al Pacino appeared on the silver screen in the title role, all of America could see the mess that was the NYPD. By that time Whitman Knapp and his commission had been hearing testimony from various cops.[6] Some of them were dirty; others, like Serpico, were trying to clean things up. The testimony painted a bleak picture of systemic corruption and criminal activity in the NYPD. The recommendations of the Knapp Commission and their implementation by the NYPD effected profound changes within the department. The corruption-riddled Plainclothes Division was scuttled and replaced by a Narcotics Division and a Public Morals Division, which fell under a new bureau called the Organized Crime Control Bureau. More significantly, the Internal Affairs Division was dramatically beefed up and given increased investigative latitude. New York City and the NYPD demonstrated their commitment to cleaning up the corruption.

The Knapp Commission, the anticorruption endeavors, and the fiscal problems of New York City cast a pall over the morale of the NYPD. As cops watched some of their partners marched out of the station house in handcuffs, the honest ones were vilified by an enraged citizenry. Paranoia and suspicion pervaded the department as more than a few police suicides rocked the collective psyche. The NYPD was reeling, not only from the corruption headlines but also from the skyrocketing crime statistics and their obvious inability to stem the tide.

The NYPD anticorruption initiatives were highly successful in rooting out the bad apples in the department. The Knapp Commission had identified the Plainclothes Division as the epicenter of systemic corruption in the department. This was attributed to the Plainclothes Division detectives and cops who handled most of the criminal activity associated with organized crime such as La Cosa Nostra or the drug trafficking organizations. For the most part, La Cosa Nostra was involved in bookmaking, gambling operations, and activities involving highjackings and selling stolen property. Although narcotics trafficking had not been a huge business in New York City, by the late 1960s things had changed and drugs were big money.[7]

Corruption and Crime

Corruption is not exclusive to cops. It is human nature and it is tough to combat. Experts have stated that it is endemic to all police departments.[8] Because plainclothesmen were constantly exposed to the criminal activities that generated a great deal of cash, they were vulnerable to corruption. For the organized criminals of La Cosa Nostra (the bookmakers and loan sharks, the numbers runners and the pimps) bribing cops was the cost of doing business. When one of these criminals was "pinched," invariably an offer was made to the cop to forget the arrest in exchange for a sum of money, usually a goodly sum. This had been going on for years, probably since the first cops and the first arrests. That doesn't make it right, but it was a reality nonetheless. Most cops would refuse the offer and go ahead with the arrest, but a greedy few would not.

As narcotics became more lucrative, so did the corruption offers to the dirty cops. It behooved the drug dealers to offer the cops larger and larger sums of cash to keep the illicit drug business in operation. As drug sentences became more severe, the bribe attempts increased in frequency and dollar amounts. Once again, it was the cost of doing business. As the money became more lucrative, the temptation became harder for cops to ignore. As more cops began taking money from the organized criminals and others, it became harder to keep the illegal payoffs secret. Soon the dirty cops were cutting in other cops on the payoffs and that is when the systematic collections, or "pads" began. The Plainclothes Division, the place where Serpico worked, became a corrupt place to work. As Serpico made clear, it was almost impossible to be an honest cop in that division. Although it is most probable that there were plenty of honest cops, there was the traditional wall of silence that prohibited these cops from coming forward. Although they were wrong to not come forward, America has never been a place that was tolerant of "rats." The Knapp Commission clearly understood and concluded, "[T]here are corrupt pads in every plainclothes gambling enforcement squad." The commission also acknowledged the same for narcotics plainclothes.[9]

Why is this history of corruption important? Although the anticorruption initiatives were successful in weeding out corruption, they had a negative effect on the department's crime-fighting capabilities. The eradication of the Plainclothes Division and the emergence of the Organized Crime Control Bureau (OCCB) significantly changed the way the NYPD battled organized crime and drug dealing. Following these changes, the only cops who could make drug and gambling arrests were the members of OCCB. An edict promulgated by the NYPD brass stated that no uniformed officers were permitted to make drug arrests. This ban was extended to numbers locations, prostitution, and bookmakers. Now these rules were not exactly spelled out on paper; they were unwritten, but certainly not unheeded. The upper echelon of the NYPD realized that the corruptive influences of organized criminal activity had to be placed beyond the reach of the street cops. They reasoned that if the temptations were removed, the street cops would be less inclined toward corruption.

That strategy was effective in one respect: It greatly reduced corruption on the patrol level. But on another level it effectively tied the uniform and plainclothes cops' hands. (There were a few plainclothes officers working in each precinct in a unit remarkably called the Anti-Crime Unit.) Once it became apparent to the street-level drug dealers, numbers runners, prostitutes, and other organized crime members that the uniform cop no longer posed a threat to their business, they became increasingly open and brazen in their business practices and criminal activity. Soon "smoke shops" were popping up, selling marijuana over the counter in many neighborhoods. Number spots became equally brazen. Street level drug sales skyrocketed as did the proliferation of cocaine and heroin. The market became more lucrative, and that's when the shootings started. Then came the turf wars. All this while the uniform cop walked the beat or drove around in what the public mistook for ignorant bliss. On the contrary, it was frustration and demoralization. The hands of the uniform cop were tied even tighter behind the back as the criminals ruled the streets of New York. The cops were effectively handcuffed.

Sensitivity Training

While crime was running rampant, the politics of policing was also changing drastically. What had started as a trickle with the firing of Broderick was now a deluge as high-level police commanders and street-level cops were subjected to increasing scrutiny by the politicians and the public for being too diligent or zealous in doing their job. Although Mayor Lindsay had not been successful in the implementation of a Civilian Review Board, the political climate had effectively transformed the media into just such an entity. Commissioner Patrick Murphy was a police commissioner who made it a point to hold supervisors responsible for any physical abuse or brutality committed by rank-and-file officers in their command. Accountability became the watchword within the department.[10] In 1973 Murphy replaced 90 percent of the top officers in the NYPD.[11]

The need for sensitivity in dealing with the public is paramount for a police officer. The use of physical force to subdue a criminal or to quell a disturbance is also a necessary tool for the police officer. It is something of a necessary evil within the occupation, and it is understood that force should be used as a last resort. Of course that is even more applicable to deadly physical force, where the strict guidelines are well established during training. These are some of the basic principles of policing for any municipality. It would take hundreds of pages to enumerate and discuss the social dynamics at work within the scope of New York City. Those dynamics, between the NYPD and the general public are visited and revisited every day in the newspapers and the media whenever allegations or evidence comes forth that a police officer has abused a citizen in the performance of duty. Sometimes the line between the necessary use of force and abuse of authority is unclear. This is an ongoing problem for New York City.

It seems that these issues came to the forefront in New York City during the waning years of Robert Wagner's administration. The shooting of 14-year-old Jimmy Powell by a white police lieutenant sparked the Harlem riot of 1964.[12] But it was the rumor circulating through the neighborhood that the victim had been unarmed that helped fan the flame from a mere confrontation into a full-blown riot.[13] It seems that was a turning point for New York City in regard to race relations and with regard to the relationship between the minority community and the NYPD. It has been a dramatic and controversial history of violence, accusation, suspicion, and allegation. It will always be so, as it will always be a work in progress, primarily because it involves the interaction of human beings who are imperfect. It is one of the most difficult issues for policing and it is only exacerbated when politicians enter into the picture for personal gain.

Lindsay may have set the tone for the policing of New York City and the issue of the use of force in the minority community, because that issue has become the proverbial political hot potato. As the demographics of New York City began to change dramatically in the late 60s and through the 80s, the issue of police brutality and the use of excessive force by a primarily white police department became increasingly important to politicians running for office or running the city. The minority community was one that, on the surface, seemed to be at odds with the police department and the way it handled problems in the community. It is difficult to gauge the breadth of a problem in those communities because of the reluctance of some members to come forward with complaints and the over-aggressive methods of some professional agitators within that community. But it would not be a stretch to say that in New York City's poorer and minority communities the NYPD never enjoyed a good reputation or rapport with those communities. In fact, *Migration News* reported that by the 1980s "eighty percent of the civilian complaints in New York City was made by non-whites. One percent led to disciplinary action."[14]

As the minority vote became increasingly important to candidates and to the mayor, so did their views on the police and police brutality. As a result, the upper echelon of the NYPD became more aware of the sensitivities within the minority communities of New York and this was passed down the line. Certainly it was a welcome development in local policing, but the implementation of sensitivity in policing was a difficult and tricky assignment. That is where the problems begin.

Accountability

The cop on the street had already been told not to make arrests for narcotics, prostitution, gambling, or anything else that might be deemed corruption prone. In fact, cops were not allowed in corruption-prone locations without a supervisor. With the advent of new sensitivity mandates, the cops and the supervisors were navigating new, dangerous, and uncharted waters. The midlevel management knew that any insensitive handling of an important or controversial special interest group might result in a reprimand or even worse, the loss of the command, and even more tragic, being forced to retire ignominiously.

One such controversial special interest group was the Hasidic Jews, whether Lubavitcher from Crown Heights or Satmar from Borough Park, Brooklyn. There may never be conclusive evidence, but anecdotally it has been established that those groups wield enormous power within their respective police precincts

Overzealousness and/or mistreatment of demonstrators and minorities on the street has been the undoing of a stellar police career, as evidenced by the abrupt firing of Assistant Chief Tom Darcy after the Tompkins Square riot erupted on the front pages of the daily tabloids and on the evening news. Darcy happened to be the ranking officer on duty when the Task Force followed the orders of their supervisors to clear the park of the protestors. Tompkins Square had always been a hotbed of political protest, and on this particular evening, reports indicated that the protestors were throwing fruit and other objects at the cops. The task force moved in and removed the demonstrators forcefully. As the story goes, Darcy was the duty chief but not on the scene of the disturbance. He didn't even give the orders. But when the video cameras captured this debacle, the mayor was embarrassed, and heads rolled. The first head to roll was Tom Darcy's. The precinct commander, Gerald McNamara, was also relieved of his command by Police Commissioner Benjamin Ward.[15]

When a local drug dealer was found to have been abused by his arresting officers in the 106th Precinct, in what has been termed the "stun gun incident," not only were those cops arrested and fired, but the precinct commander was brought up on charges, the borough commander was forced to resign, and the Chief of Patrol retired. That is accountability in the NYPD. The man sent to the 106th Precinct to clean things up wound up becoming the police commissioner in 1992, Raymond Kelly. And it is Ray Kelly who may best understand and explain the undercurrent or culture of passivity that gripped the NYPD on the eve of the Crown Heights riot and during the weeks' tumultuous events.

A Culture of Passivity

In a *New York Magazine* article from 2003, Kelly explains in detail the mindset of the NYPD in those dark days:

> He was even more surprised by the passive posture of the police.
>
> "No tactics were being used to control the situation," Kelly, now the police commissioner, told me recently. "The police were essentially just standing there looking at the crowd. And you'd see these kids run out suddenly and throw something at the cops ... It wasn't smart policing."[16]

Kelly had been the commanding officer of the 71st Precinct in the mid 1980s, and was actually sent from the 71st to clean up the 106th Precinct in the wake of the "stun gun" incident. Now in 1991 Kelly was standing on familiar ground. Again he asked to clean up the problem. In the *New York Magazine* article Craig Horowitz explained how Kelly had been outside the uniform chain of command even though at the time he was the First Deputy Commissioner. In that capacity Kelly eventually stepped forward and took control of the situation. Aggressive police tactics were adopted, arrests followed, and by Thursday things were coming under control.

Kelly also addressed the question as to whether an order was ever given to hold back. Kelly felt there may have been a culture of passivity regarding commanders reluctant to take any radical steps that might not be in line with what the mayor or his administration may have wanted. But this was all perception. The perception most commanders wanted to avoid was that of an over-reactive, predominantly white police force using force to quell a group of black demonstrators.

In a few short paragraphs Ray Kelly addressed the issue at hand for the NYPD, a climate that pervaded the management and to some extent the rank-and-file. Without pointing fingers or speculating on the cause of such a climate, Kelly made it clear that there was executive paralysis in the NYPD and there was little or no guidance from City Hall.

Many political observers point to the Crown Heights Riot as the catalyst for the election of Rudy Giuliani in 1993. In an article titled "The Crown Heights Pogrom," Fred Siegel asserts: "The city was on the brink of social dissolution. The situation led to then Mayor Dinkins' downfall and the election of Giuliani."[17] Whether hyperbole or astute political analysis, Siegel points out that Giuliani took over a city where crime was king and the citizen was cowering in his home. In a few short years that dynamic would change drastically and dramatically. It is startling how simple the solution was.

Bratton, Maple, and Compstat

On taking office Giuliani promptly made a major change in the NYPD. By promoting William Bratton to police commissioner, Guiliani was turning to a relative outsider for help. Although Bratton had been the chief of the New York Transit Police Department in the early 1990s, he had originally come from Boston where he served as the Chief of Police. Going outside the department was not a radical departure, but it certainly had not worked when David Dinkins tapped Lee Brown as his commissioner. Brown had come highly credentialed from Houston where he was the police commissioner, but Brown never seemed to get a grasp on the crime problem in New York and when he left office the city was in shambles. Bratton had his own views on the NYPD that he later shared in books and articles, such as this one called "What We Learned from Policing":

> The only way you can control a police department from headquarters is if your aim is to prevent police from doing anything ... and for many years that was precisely the aim of the NYPD. ... Accordingly, cops became more cautious as they rose in rank, right up to the highest levels.[18]

Bratton had a reputation as a no-nonsense commander, a man who had made some significant changes to the Transit Police during his regime. He had campaigned for better weapons for the transit cops and won. That improved morale and helped the cops do their job. He had implemented some new and innovative crime-fighting techniques that had worked wonders in the subways. Some of those innovations were the product of a veteran transit police lieutenant named Jack Maple, who has been hailed as an eccentric visionary within law enforcement circles.

Some of Maple's ideas were radical and some of them were merely common sense, but one of his innovations has made a profound effect on policing in the United States. It is a process called Compstat, an acronym of sorts for computer statistics. Simply stated, Compstat is the charting of crime stats within a precinct, a borough, or a city, and addressing those statistics with manpower and strategic initiatives. Compstat meetings are conferences in which the monthly crime statistics are presented to the commander of a particular precinct and then that commander is asked how he is addressing those problems. The Compstat conferences became the board meetings of the NYPD with the commissioner and the chiefs posing the tough questions and calling their commanders on the carpet. Compstat really was another method of accountability: What was a commander doing to lower the crime stats in his or her precinct? It was simple but revolutionary. In the late 1990s law enforcement officials from all over the world would attend Compstat conferences held by the NYPD.

There's a New Sheriff in Town

Another revolutionary yet simple notion was espoused by Rudy Giuliani himself; let the cops be cops and do their jobs! Some have called it the broken window theory of law enforcement and others called it bottom feeding, but the premise was to allow a cop to take action whenever and wherever the law was broken. That meant street cops arresting drug dealers, transit cops arresting fare beaters, and it meant petty criminals finding themselves in jail for crimes they used to get away with. There would be no more skating. In the first six months of Giuliani's term, the NYPD locked everybody up, and put most of those people in jail for at least a couple of hours. Some of the arrests were called quality-of-life arrests and were put through the jail system over night. Heretofore these arrests were mere slaps on the wrist, but under Giuliani the perpetrators were going to jail for a while and paying fines.

Those were controversial times, because civilian complaints, primarily from the minority community were on the rise, but they signified the beginning of a new regime and a new war on crime, a war that New York City was beginning to win. By the mid 1990s the results were in and the crime stats were down, the city was definitely a safer place in which to live, play, or visit.[19] While there were myriad reasons for this, those early initiatives by Giuliani clearly were part of the sea change. To most observers, Giuliani was willing to live with the civilian complaints and potential corruption issues in order to significantly reduce crime. But what also must be taken into account is the catalyst for that change; the recognition by Ray Kelly that a passive police department meant an ineffective police department. And as Ray Kelly realized this, so did many of the citizens of New York City who created a sea change of their own. They had turned David Dinkins out of the City Hall and replaced him with a Republican mayor named Rudy Giuliani. The results have been startling.

In the 1980s it would have been unthinkable that a Republican would occupy Gracie Mansion for 20 uninterrupted years, but when Michael Bloomberg completes his term in 2013, that will be the case. It also would have been unthinkable in those desperate 1980s and 90s that the murder rate in New York City in 2005 would be lower than it was in 1964, but that is also the case. Maybe it took a return to some of the practices of those years, along with the incorporation of some modern techniques. It is a controversial theory of policing, but in New York City it seems to be working.

CHAPTER 14

NOBODY OWNS A NEIGHBORHOOD

Nobody owns a neighborhood. Not an ethnic group, not a race, not a religious group. In New York City, neighborhoods are like transfer stations on a subway line. Except for the richest neighborhoods—Fifth Avenue and Central Park West—almost every neighborhood changes. Some of the exclusive neighborhoods have been handed down to the poor. We have recently seen how even the poorest neighborhoods, some with severe crime problems, suddenly become the darling of the young urban professionals and are soon gentrified. Soon the people who grew up in the neighborhood can't afford to live there. It happened in Harlem, it happened on the lower east side of Manhattan, and it's happening in downtown Brooklyn, in Williamsburg and Greenpoint.

The neighborhoods are in a constant state of flux. Sure, a group might dominate a neighborhood for a while, even a few decades. But we have found that eventually all things must pass. You don't have to tell that to the Irish, Italian, and Jewish residents of Crown Heights who ran to the outer borough of Queens and to Long Island, as an influx of new immigrants arrived one day in the late 1950s. This time the new immigrant was a Caribbean Black from Jamaica or Haiti, or perhaps an American Black arriving with the Great Migration from the south. It didn't really matter where they came from or who they were, it was their turn. That is New York City, Brooklyn, and in some sense, America.

But if any neighborhood was dominated by a group, it may have been Crown Heights. From its earliest days it was inhabited by black people. Most of them were freed slaves or simply free men and women who had come from Manhattan or from nearby Weeksville-Carrsville. They lived in the area when it was called Crow Hill and they remained for the better part of two centuries. Eventually they were usurped by other ethnic groups as the newly named Crown Heights became a more desirable address, but in some vestige Blacks were always in Crown Heights.

So in some respect it must have been a little disconcerting for the majority black population of Crown Heights to watch as a new immigrant group arrived in their neighborhood. Perhaps this is a rite of passage for each ethnic group that finally gets a foothold in America. They watch as a lower group on the immigration-societal totem pole moves into their neighborhood and begins to take the houses that were vacated by members of their own group who have moved up and out. It happened to the Irish and the Jews and the Italians all over the city. In Crown Heights however there was a different dynamic at work.

In some respects the Blacks had yet to move up to the next level. In fact, Crown Heights had been a step up for many of the Caribbean immigrants and for quite a few of the American Blacks migrating from Bedford-Stuyvesant. Crown Heights had become their new neighborhood, where they had put down roots and bought homes. But it was not yet the suburbs. For many in the neighborhood it was a start not a destination. When the Lubavitcher Hasidic Jews began arriving in larger numbers in the mid to late 1960s it was a rude awakening to the black population.

All of a sudden there was a battle for housing, and not necessarily for desirable housing. The neighborhood was old and some of the buildings were dilapidated and decrepit. Many of the landlords had been in a panic over the black influx at the end of the 1950s. Many of those landlords had become "slumlords." The arrival of the Hasidim created a minor housing market in what was considered a bad neighborhood. And that was the problem. There shouldn't be competition for housing in what people mistakenly refer to as "the ghetto." But there was competition and the Blacks resented the fact that in many instances the Lubavitchers were beating them to the punch. It was more exasperating that this was happening with the blessing of City Hall and the Democratic Party. After all, the Blacks were big supporters of the party, too.

The housing problem was only one of many, as the Lubavitchers came to dominate the school board even though their children did not attend public school. Finally, the redistricting and creation of Community Board #9 was one of the last straws. The extra police protection and the motorcades made things worse.

All of this was obvious to any working cop in Brooklyn, especially in Crown Heights. That is where the protests were and that is where the problems were. How could City Hall and the Democratic Party not see this? The answer is that they didn't want to see it. They certainly did see it, but were faced with a conundrum. How could they not answer the phone when the rebbe or his emissary called and asked for a political favor? The answer was that they couldn't say no. The Democratic leadership of New York City continued to throw money at the problem hoping that it would go away. But things got continuously worse. By the time David Dinkins took office it was hopeless.

The election of Dinkins offered hope to his own people, the Blacks, and in many ways he delivered. But in Crown Heights things remained the same. Dinkins had his own core group but he was also a Democratic machine politician and he had to toe the line. Or at least he couldn't rock the boat.

But Al Sharpton, Herb Daughtry, and Sonny Carson weren't faced with the same restraints. So they rocked the boat, protesting all over Bedford-Stuyvesant, Crown Heights, and especially at the Korean market boycott on Church Avenue; the precursor to the Crown Heights riot. Dinkins couldn't control them. He couldn't control them during the boycott and he couldn't control them during the heavy days of the riot. That was obvious. David Dinkins was a politician caught in the middle and was not prepared to handle the problem.

The writing of a book is a journey. Most people embarking on a journey usually have some expectation of what the destination might look like. Others do not. Sometimes a person will arrive at their destination and not recognize it because it is not what they expected. In some respects that is the case with the Crown Heights Riot of 1991. Sometimes the author or investigator is taken to unexpected places. With this project, I had a pretty good idea of what Crown Heights was about. I had been there extensively and I knew the people on both sides. While I had a few preconceived notions, for the most part I felt open minded.

I knew that I would never be able to prove that David Dinkins and his administration told the police to back off and "let the crowd vent." I knew it because I was reasonably sure that it most likely did not happen. And if it did happen there would be plausible deniability. But I also believed that Dinkins would never have wanted to see anyone, Jew or Black or cop, get hurt or killed. I believed he was a decent and honest man, and I still believe it. People have told me he was arrogant, and I believe that could be true. But that is no crime, just a character flaw.

But I initially felt that Dinkins mishandled the whole situation. And that is one of my conclusions. David Dinkins didn't intentionally allow the rioting to rage for four days, it happened because of inexperience and lack of leadership. He allowed the ship to founder, That ship being the NYPD. The Girgenti Commission put the onus on the Police Department, blaming the field commanders for not being proactive and taking care of business. But the police didn't allow Crown Heights to rage out of control, the politicians did—both before the riot and while it raged. How? By effectively tying the hands of the police for 30 years. Dinkins just happened to be in charge when Crown Heights happened. He shares the blame along with Lindsay, Beame, and Koch, his predecessors who decided that there could be an acceptable level of lawlessness in New York City in what they felt were the interests of racial harmony. But it was really in the interests of political expedience. By allowing crime to proliferate, by telling cops to use a hands off policy in the "bad neighborhoods" these politicians were feeding the honest and good citizens of the bad neighborhoods to the wolves. Perhaps these bad neighborhoods were only bad because the politicians allowed them to get that way.

There is a scene in the film *Fort Apache, The Bronx* that epitomizes this situation and philosophy. Paul Newman starred as a washed-up and discouraged NYPD cop working in the worst neighborhood in the Bronx, Fort Apache, the nickname for the 41st Precinct during the 1970s. A new commander, played by a gruff and straight-laced Ed Asner, came to the command and turned things upside down. He made the cops go out and do their job, the cops arrested everyone committing crimes, even minor ones, and as a result a minor riot ensued outside the station house.

While the riot was raging, Newman, the discouraged and cynical cop, asked captain Asner if he still felt it was all worth it. Asner's reply was prescient and maybe the most sound advice never to be used in New York City. Asner replied to his jaded subordinate that there were good and decent people in that hell-hole of a precinct, and they had to know that the law was still the law. And it would be enforced to protect those people. That is why cops do their jobs every day.

But the politicians in New York City made it difficult for the good cops to do their jobs every day. Thirty years of hands-off policy had emboldened drug dealers, robbers, and society's other miscreants. The instructions by Dinkins' Police Commissioner Lee P. Brown to his commanders was that they should go out and "make friends with your enemies."[1] The idea that a career could be jeopardized by zealousness had a chilling effect on the entire police department. What developed was a culture of passivity. The cop was told to check with a supervisor before taking action. Not only in a riot but in most situations on the street. Each supervisor checked with the one above. It had a disabling effect. When Ray Powers said that his phone was ringing only a few minutes after he took the bullhorn from Coltrane Chimurenga, he wasn't surprised. This was not unusual. So when it came time to make a decision in Crown Heights, it is not surprising that there was a vacuum of leadership.

Assistant Chief Thomas Gallagher knew what to do and how to do it. But what he needed was some direction from City Hall. Any action without direction would be career suicide. For Gallagher, that's how it turned out anyway. But the lack of police action was disturbing.

The people who were calling 911 on those violent and frightening days and nights in August 1991 were not only Jewish or Lubavitcher. They were Black and Hispanic and most likely many other ethnicities and races. Crime does not discriminate. Although the Jews were the initial targets of the rioters' rage, quickly it degenerated into an antipolice or an antigovernment riot. After all, it was the government that had been so accommodating to the Lubavitchers, and the police were the representatives of the government in the street. Then it degenerated into mayhem and anarchy.

Was it a pogrom? Maybe it was a pogrom for a few minutes for a few people. For the most part there were anti-Semitic undertones to the riot, and the initial reaction was most certainly anti-Semitic, but the brunt of the attacks changed quickly. Most of the stores looted were on Utica Avenue and not on Kingston Avenue, which is the Jewish shopping district. This is partly because Kingston Avenue was highly protected, but it is also a coincidence of circumstances. The riot started on Utica and that became ground zero for violence and protest. The looting was just old-fashioned crime happening at an opportune time. And the victims on Utica Avenue, the store owners, were as ethnically and racially diverse as David Dinkins' "gorgeous mosaic."

While the Girgenti Commission was busy blaming the Police Department, it seemed to miss certain opportunities to really find out what was happening on the streets during the riot. Ray Powers was not interviewed by the commission. That is a startling revelation. When he told me this, I was stunned. Here was a police captain who had spent the better part of 10 years on the streets in that neighborhood. He knew all the players, both Lubavitcher and Black. Powers also knew what happened out there those violent nights, but the commission neglected to interview him.

Although it is an extensive report, it obviously was not comprehensive enough. The omission of Powers borders on willful negligence. In actuality it seems as if maybe the commission was carefully choosing the sources of its information. This is only speculation. The commission report occasionally quotes actors in the riot, but much of the information is not directly attributed, and as a result, the veracity of the information is suspect. There are other notable omissions in the report. It is surprising that the present police commissioner, Ray Kelly, was not interviewed or cited as a source in the report and, likewise, the current Chief of Department, Joseph Esposito, who had a very significant role as a street commander. Once again, they may have been interviewed but the information is not directly attributed, so how viable is the information? It seems that the Girgenti Commission may have been afraid of what it might find and, therefore, limited the scope of the investigation.

While the NYPD and the Dinkins Administration shared in the blame, there is another glaring omission. The purveyors of the politics of confrontation: the Revs. Daughtry and Sharpton; the lawyers Moore, Maddox, and Mason; and the activists Carson, Chimurenga, and the New York 8. This loosely affiliated group of political activists, whom some people describe as demagogues and rabble rousers, had been agitating in the neighborhood for the better part of a decade. Sharpton's sun had almost set with the Tawana Brawley fiasco but somehow he managed to revive his career as an activist looking for an issue. The dubiousness of Sharpton is complemented by Carson, Chimurenga, and the New York 8, who constantly seemed to be in search of confrontation and situations that might lead to tension-filled stand-offs. Daughtry seems to be the most responsible and bona fide representative of the black community of this whole group, and his defense of his role entitled *No Monopoly on Suffering*, illustrated the long-standing problems and issues in Crown Heights and New York City.

But issues and complaints, no matter how valid or frustrating, are no justification for violence. Daughtry and the activists did not start the violence. That seemed to be a spontaneous eruption from a frustrated and irate community. But the activists poured into the area at the immediate outbreak of violence and basically did nothing to ease the situation or soothe the riotous crowd. On the contrary, the organized marches and protests seemed to become breeding grounds for violent thugs looking to use the situation for their own sinister or misguided agendas. Daughtry and the group may not have intended for their protests to prolong and exacerbate the riot, but they certainly did not heed Mayor Dinkins' requests to curtail their activities in the interest of peace and harmony. The media jumped on this, but the Girgenti Commission just about ignored it. It is an important component of the riot. These people bear responsibility for their public actions. Enjoying the role of spokesmen for a group—racial, religious, or ethnic—must come with some civic responsibility, which was not exercised by this group. But as often happens in New York politics, they were let off the hook.

Finally, the other victims of the riot must take their own share of the blame. While the Lubavitcher is a largely law-abiding segment of the community, there have been instances over the years of racially motivated violence against certain members of the black community in Crown Heights. In addition, it has always been obvious, to almost everyone, that there was always a certain amount of contempt within the Hasidic community for the surrounding neighbors. The dominance of New York City politics tells some of that story: the 24x7 police protection and the motorcades. It was incumbent on the Lubavitchers to attempt a compromise with their neighbors, to arrive at some sort of state of peaceful coexistence. It had been evident that, although the Lubavitchers have participated in community programs and councils, for the most part, they preferred to keep to themselves. They do not want assimilation.

The term melting pot came into our collective consciousness in 1926 when the curtain went up on Israel Zangwill's play *The Melting Pot*. The story of a Jewish immigrant and his quest for acceptance and success in America, the play was not highly regarded but the term took on a life of its own. Many people feel that it has come to describe our society. In *Beyond the Melting Pot*, Nathan Glazer and Daniel Patrick Moynihan's ground-breaking treatise on New York City race and ethnic relations, the authors arrived at the conclusion that the term melting pot is in, fact, a misnomer. They maintain that it does not exist because there is no actual melting. The different ethnic and racial groups exist side-by-side in proximity, but they do not necessarily merge. Eventually they become Americanized, but retain their ethnic and racial essence.

That very well may be the story of the Lubavitcher Hasidim in America. They are searching for their own village, the insular place they inhabited in Eastern Europe before and during the pogroms. They do not want to assimilate because assimilation would mean the destruction of their culture. An ironic parallel is the Muslim community in America. Assimilation is not necessarily a desirable goal. In Crown Heights, the Lubavitchers have assembled their own village in the midst of a larger black community. They do not necessarily want to be part of that community yet they have figured out how to maneuver the tricky political streets of New York City, and they have used it to their significant advantage. But that advantage turned into a liability, and just like the riots that took place in Russia and the Cossack revolt, the neighborhood turned against the Lubavitchers. It may not be right, it certainly is not an acceptable means of political expression, and it is tragic, but the riot continues to hold its place in American history as a wake-up call. In Crown Heights the riot of 1991 was a harsh and deadly awakening for the Lubavitcher Hasidim and for the Democratic Party of New York City that allowed the situation to deteriorate to the point of combustion. How could anyone not hold the Democratic Party leadership responsible for what happened during its nearly three-decade reign in New York City? Certainly the buck must stop somewhere. But, just as in the fallout of the financial crisis of the mid 1970s, there seems to be a reluctance to accept responsibility.

In the aftermath of the riot, it appears that the Lubavitchers have learned their lessons to some degree. They have taken a more active role in community outreach programs and it appears that they have, to a certain extent, distanced themselves from the Democratic Party, or at least David Dinkins, who himself blames the Lubavitchers for his fall from grace. In a *New York Times* article from 1995 Joyce Purnick explained: "The Hasidim of Crown Heights are unforgiving of his handling of the 1991 Crown Heights Riots because of his race. 'It's pure racism,' said the man who has at times refused to use the r-word."[2] But the Democratic Party suffers right along with Dinkins as it hasn't been able to put a candidate in the mayor's office in 16 years. In those 16 years crime has plummeted and quality of life is arguably much improved, as has the economy. As a result it would appear that a violent and tragic eruption in Crown Heights may have significantly changed the future of New York City. That flashpoint in a melting pot became a watershed for New York City.

CHAPTER 15 THE POLICE AND THE COMMUNITY

ACCOUNTABILITY

When Lee Brown retired from public service in 2006, he left behind a substantial legacy of success in a storied career in law enforcement. It was a career that spawned four decades and many major cities in the United States. Considered the "father of community policing," Brown's commitment to Community Oriented Policing (COP) and his success in implementing that strategy in Houston is what paved his path to New York City. But it was in New York City that Brown's career and his strategies encountered some major turbulence.

Brown's abrupt departure from the Big Apple in 1992 raised many unanswered questions regarding the actual success of Community Oriented Policing as an urban law enforcement strategy. After leaving New York City, Lee Brown eventually served two terms as mayor of Houston, the scene of his greatest professional success. But his impressive résumé points to his short stint as New York City police commissioner as one of many high points in what has been hailed as a celebrated career. Unfortunately the data does not support this. Even more troubling is the apparent willingness on the part of many politicians to overlook or gloss over the fact that Brown's tenure as NYC police commissioner featured the return of rioting to the city, with the Crown Heights Riots followed the next summer by a smaller, but no less violent riot in Washington Heights. They were the first riots in NYC since 1964.

The riots during Brown's regime coupled with the horrendous crime statistics, particularly the murder rate, should lead any unbiased observer to conclude that Brown's strategies were unsuccessful. Again, it appears that revisionist history has attempted to put rose-colored glasses on the "gorgeous mosaic," or, to be colloquial, lipstick on a pig. A perusal of the Democrats.org website for February 2011 features a Lee Brown résumé that includes New York City as one of his triumphs. Perhaps now is the time to set that record straight.

When David Dinkins was elected mayor of New York City, he promised a healing administration, one that would bring together a divided society. Naturally one of the most significant problems facing Dinkins was a surging crime rate. This crime rate had been rising inexorably since 1964 for a variety of reasons. Dinkins, in appointing Lee Brown, told the people of New York City that Community Oriented Policing would be the answer to their problems. The police would reach out to the community and begin to find a way to work out the problems. Brown's programs had been successful in Atlanta and more recently in Houston, and Dinkins was betting that Brown would continue to experience that success here in the Big Apple.

But Brown's programs and strategies did not seem to take hold. Community policing had been introduced in NYC during Ben Ward's six years as police commissioner, and the word on the street and within the rank and file was that the program was not working. The CPOP (Community Police on Patrol) units were viewed by the street cops as "just another detail that got you off patrol." The patrol cops riding in the radio cars felt that the CPOP cops had found an easy niche, a place where they enjoyed steady day tours and didn't have to pick up the radio. Some of those sentiments were true. On the other hand, it had been proven in other cities that community policing strategies were helpful to police departments in gaining the trust of the community. Experts like Herman Goldstein had been extolling the virtues and benefits of these new strategies. Goldstein, a renowned professor of law at the University of Wisconsin, looked to community policing as a revolutionary change, a more intelligent and responsive approach to working with and within a community:

> The new policing seeks to make the police job more achievable by realigning what the police do and do not do by giving higher priority to some tasks and lower priority to others, by reducing public expectations and leveling with the public about police capacity, by engaging the public in taking steps to help themselves, and by connecting with other agencies and the private sector in ways that ensure that citizens referred to them will be helped. There is a need to invest much more, in our individual communities, in working through the questions that arise in trying to achieve this better alignment.[1]

But there was no statistical evidence to suggest that CPOP strategies were working in New York City. In fact, crime was up. The crack wars were a significant problem on the streets of New York, as the murder rate continued to rise through the late 1980s and into the 90s. More horrifying to city residents was the collateral damage of these turf wars: the high number of innocent bystanders getting shot and killed, many of them children.

The Dinkins apologists tell us that the mayor and his police commissioner began to address these issues and were beginning to experience limited success. The party line has it that Dinkins initiated a program called Safe Streets, Safe Cities, and that the subsequent increase in manpower helped the New York City Police Department begin its historic reduction in the crime rate. While there is some truth to that story, history and the crime statistics tell us that it is only a small part of the picture.

While it is true that the Dinkins Administration was responsible for the initiation of Safe Streets, Safe Cities in NYC, and the subsequent increase in police manpower, there was not a significant reduction in crime during his administration. To simply say that Safe Streets began the reduction would be disingenuous. Many experts agree that the increased manpower was a step in the right direction, but almost all the experts maintain that it was a dramatic change in crime fighting strategy that created a climate in which crime fell at historic rates. And that strategy was called Compstat.

YEAR	MURDER	ROBBERY	ASSAULT	BURGLARY	PAGE
1994	1,561	72,540	59,775	88,370	p. 138
1993	1,946	86,001	62,778	99,207	p. 139
1992	1,995	91,239	63,529	103,476	p. 141
1991	2,154	98,512	66,832	112,015	p. 139
1990	2,245	100,280	68,891	119,937	p. 101
1989	1,905	93,377	70,951	121,322	p. 101
1988	1,896	86,578	71,030	127,148	p. 101

Source: FBI unified crime reports

Regime Change, New York City Style

Lee Brown resigned in October 1992, and Dinkins named Ray Kelly, one of the heroes of Crown Heights, to succeed him as police commissioner. In many ways, the ascension of Kelly to the police commissioner's job was the fulfillment of a prophecy. To anyone who worked for Kelly in the 7-1 (the 71st Precinct), it was only a matter of time before he was elevated to that he called his "dream job." The 7-1 alumni were not alone in cheering Kelly's arrival on the scene, because he brought with him the insight and experience of a man who had worked "the job" from the bottom up. He had the résumé and the know-how; good things appeared on the horizon.

But politically, for Dinkins anyway, the damage was done. Although the election of 1993 would be just as close as 1989, this time the results would be reversed. Through no fault of his own, Kelly basically was serving out the last year of a lame duck mayor. Kelly's early initiatives held much promise, but there was not enough time. Additionally, the crime issues were not receding very much. Although there was a reduction in the index crimes, it was hardly noticeable. The Unified Crime Reports compiled by the FBI tell the crime story of the Dinkins administration and perhaps that of Lee Brown, as well. In 1988, the year before Dinkins' election to mayor, there were 1,896 murders in New York City. In the election year, 1989, there was only an increase of 9 homicides. But in 1990, following Dinkins' and Brown's first year in power, murders increased to 2,245. That was 340 more people killed in one year in New York City than under Ed Koch. The number decreased slightly in 1991 when *only* 2,154 people were murdered in the city. The ensuing years saw a reduction of about 50 fewer murders a year in 1992 and 1993, but these numbers were not significant enough to herald a sea change. The murder rate fell off the continental shelf in 1994 when the Giuliani administration announced that the murders in the city had plummeted to 1,561, a decrease of 385.[2] A sea change indeed was about to occur. But the change agent would not be community oriented policing. A new era of policing was about to be ushered in, and it would revolve around a crime-fighting strategy called Compstat.

The Compstat Era

The election of Rudy Giuliani in 1993 should have been the handwriting on the wall for Ray Kelly. But nobody could blame him if he couldn't read it. Many believed that Giuliani would keep Kelly as the police commissioner. Some cited the fact that they had both attended Manhattan College and they weren't far apart in years or ideology. And Kelly was a quintessential New Yorker, just like Giuliani. But when he named William Bratton as his new police commissioner, a jilted Kelly opted for a successful career in federal law enforcement, first commanding the multi-national force in Haiti and then serving as under secretary of the U.S. Treasury.

The promotion of Bratton to police commissioner was the watershed moment for New York City. It was as if a breath of fresh air—no, a stiff wind—blew through One Police Plaza. Bratton already had a great reputation from his stint as the Chief of the Transit Police, and as a result, many cops were looking forward to his return at the helm of the big job. It doesn't happen very often, but in this case, Bratton and company exceeded the wildest expectations of even the most optimistic cops. And a lot of it had to do with that one word: Compstat.

As the crime statistics illustrated, Community Oriented Policing could not be called a success. And it certainly was not for lack of trying. Lee Brown was considered to be a pioneer in this strategy, and he himself felt that New York City was just the right place for COP to flourish:

From *The New York Times*:

In announcing his resignation, it was clear that Mr. Brown wanted to be remembered for his work on community policing, calling New York City a place that is "made for community policing" because it can be tailored to address the needs of different neighborhoods.

"My agenda was clear," he said yesterday. "To implement a new style of policing, a new way of delivering services to the people of this great city.[3]

But it was certainly unclear was whether community policing could be called a success at all. Judging by the Unified Crime Reports it most definitely could not. But that did not stop the accolades from pouring in.

From *The New York Times*:

"The great accomplishment of Lee Brown is that he got us off and running on community policing," said Thomas A. Reppetto, who as head of the Citizens Crime Commission has watched and assessed many police administrations. "If he stayed and was successful, it would have gone down in history books on law enforcement. That work has to be carried on by somebody else.[4]

That work would be carried on by Bill Bratton and his crew. In any event, Lee Brown left town, and Ray Kelly actually appeared to make some headway against the rising tide of violent crime. In 1993, Kelly's last year as police commissioner under Dinkins, all the index crimes decreased. But the sea change was about to occur on somebody else's watch.

When Rudy Giuliani was sworn in as 107th mayor of New York, he promised a new era and some radical changes. By virtue of the fact that a Republican was taking over Gracie Mansion, New York City had already experienced seismic shocks to the political landscape, (although many politicos would point to the fact that, like New York's last Republican mayor, Rudy had once been a Democrat and was not terribly conservative). But what was going to happen next would exceed New York City's wildest dreams. By the end of Giuliani's first term, the murder rate would plummet, as would the index crimes, to incredibly low levels. And, at the end of Rudy's two terms as mayor of New York City, the crime rate had sunk below that of 1964, a year that was once described as the "last innocent year." How did this happen?

Giuliani's new era began with the appointment of William Bratton as police commissioner. As a relative outsider Bratton wasn't restricted by an old boy network or the price of loyalty and the burden of honoring a plethora of insider contracts. But his stint as Chief of the Transit Police Department had afforded Bratton more than a glimpse of the inner workings of the NYPD and City Hall, so the new police commissioner was ready with his own agenda. It certainly helped that the man residing in Gracie Mansion had campaigned on a law and order platform, and law and order would be the springboard to success.

Of all the moves William Bratton made as police commissioner of New York City, perhaps the most important was the appointment of the eccentric Jack Maple as his Deputy Commissioner of Crime Strategies. Maple burnished an image of arrogance and oddity, best evidence by his haute haberdashery. But inside the ostentatious wardrobe lurked the mind and soul of a street cop. Perhaps Maple himself put it best in his tome, *The Crime Fighter*:

> The cop who decides to be a crime fighter has a tough road. To begin with, an active cop creates problems for his bosses. A tour with no arrests is an easy tour for the boss, but every arrest that's made means added paperwork and an added risk that some of the paperwork might be wrong. It means having to worry about a prisoner—his meals, his visits to the bathroom, and whether he gets smacked by the cop assigned to watch the cell or gets left alone and tries to hang himself in the cell. And because an arrest can take many hours to process, it means fielding questions from the captain about why the tour is running up overtime. When the crime fighter takes a prisoner downtown for arraignment there are no welcoming parades.[5]

Maple had spent a career working the subways and the streets, and, more important, formulating strategies that would result in increased arrests. He viewed himself as a crime fighter, but he was a street cop with a chip on his shoulder. Although he had risen to the rank of lieutenant in the Transit Police, he recognized and even prided himself on his role as an outsider. He wore on his sleeve all the slights and innuendos of years spent, as he put it, trying to crash the party.

> I was forty-one in 1993 when I finally got a seat at the table. I had been a cop since about the time I was first allowed to walk into a bar unaccompanied by an adult, but in the very profession that had consumed most of my life, I had until that year been very much on the outside, my cheeks red from the cold and my nosed pressed up against the window. In New York City, there were separate police forces for the streets, the subways and public housing,

> but only one had manpower equal to the fifth largest army in the world and a reputation equal to the New York Yankees. I was with one of the other two. In the eyes of the world, Transit was junior varsity. Transit was Naugahyde.[6]

Maple was frustrated by the years he spent working the streets, getting to know the crime hotspots, and developing a fundamental understanding of crime in New York, only to have the bigwigs of the NYPD shoo him away from the table.[7] He took it personally, but it also provided the drive that would put him in position to implement his own strategies.

Maple had spent years "in the hole," watching perps, making collars, and supervising decoy squads. He had an inherent understanding of how, why, and where crime was happening. He had developed extensive methodologies of policing. Community policing did not fit into Maple's methodologies. Although Maple never brought up objections or resistance to community policing strategies, he believed that his initiatives, supported by community policing would be successful. For one thing, he felt that community policing was an expensive proposition that most municipalities couldn't afford:

> '[C]ommunity policing,' an idea that truly could make every city in America a safer place—if Americans everywhere were willing to double or triple the size of their police forces and if police executives everywhere were ready to admit they've been faking its implementation almost since it was dreamed up.[8]

When Bratton was the chief of the New York City Transit PD he had encountered Maple and developed an appreciation for Maple's knowledge, research, and crime fighting theories. Maple had caught his ear and the Transit PD began implementing the strategies. The results came almost instantaneously. When Bratton left for the greener pastures back to his hometown of Boston he brought Maple with him. But now Bratton was back in the Big Apple and Jack Maple was sitting at his right hand, poised to take a big bite.

Jack Maple's bite of the Big Apple would become legendary. The strategies that came to be called Compstat involved many of the theories and the methodology he had honed as a crime-fighter in the Transit Police department. His methods were tried-and-true. The results were readily available, which was one of the reasons why Bratton hobnobbed with the roly-poly lieutenant decked out in white spats and a homburg hat! But now the Transit lieutenant held the title of Deputy Commissioner of Crime Control Strategies. He was no longer looking in the window; he was now sitting at the table, commanding respect, demanding respect.

Using a Batman analogy, Maple explained:

> "You know," I said, "I met some of these chiefs at the Christmas tree lighting at Rockefeller Center, and I heard a few of their chuckles when Bratton told them I was going to be his crime guy. But inside, I'm smiling like [Jack] Nicholson, and I'm thinking, 'Wait till they get a load of me.'[9]

The first order of business was to shake up the status quo. Because of crime, New York City was the national punch line. Nobody appeared to be safe, and few people felt safe. Maple was about to transfer that feeling into the management of the NYPD.

The watchword for Compstat, the fundamental operational strategy that made Compstat almost an immediate success, was accountability. Bratton and Maple and the new Chief of Department, John Timoney, understood that things had to be shaken up. The old methods had not worked for a long time. It was time to implement changes, and the most profound of those changes would come to be called the "Compstat Meeting." The meetings, which took place with great regularity, would become legendary in the annals of the NYPD, because it was at these meetings that the top brass of the department, the Chief of the Department, the Deputy Commissioner for Crime Strategies, and sometimes the commissioner himself would call a precinct commander or a borough commander on the carpet and have him explain why his precinct or his borough was not making any headway with crime. It only took one or two meetings where the word filtered out that everybody in the room—Inspectors, Deputy Inspectors, Captains and Lieutenants—shifted uncomfortably in their seats while they watched a fellow precinct commander or even a one-star chief stand at the podium and wilt under the intensive interrogation of Maple and Timoney and later, Chief of Department, Louie Annemone.

The top brass were asking the hard questions, and the commander had better have some good answers. Because the next thing anyone knew, the commander was listening, mouth agape, as Maple told that commander exactly what the numbers reflected in that man's own precinct. The big bosses started asking questions about specific cases and patterns that were happening in that precinct. How did they know these things? Maple and crew had assembled their own investigative teams that went out to the precincts and boroughs and gathered statistics and information and looked at specific case folders (and of course these investigators were much resented). Armed with this information, they could now focus attention on a specific case, ask a detective squad boss why there had not been an arrest of a named perpetrator in a robbery case. Unless a commander was the greatest of tap dancers, the only way to survive the dreaded Compstat meetings was to have the answers.

And that was the answer Maple, Bratton, Giuliani, and ultimately, New York City needed! Accountability. Now the borough commander was being grilled about a crime pattern in a precinct within his borough. Now a detective squad boss was being called on the carpet about a string or pattern of robberies happening in the precinct. Had they made an arrest on that open homicide in which the perp was named? If not, why not? These were hard questions. But the men and women of the NYPD were resourceful and resilient. The bosses knew they needed the answers, and most often the answers required an arrest or many arrests. So the bosses turned the cops loose. Necessity being the mother of invention, new street-level strategies were being devised, and soon it was no longer fun to be a perp in New York City. In 1994, Giuliani's first year as mayor, murders decreased by 20 percent, which at the time seemed to be an amazing development. By the end of the second year the murder rate had plummeted by 50 percent!

What had changed? Criminologists, sociologists, political scientists, and just about every other political pundit looked around for some reason why this happened. Demographic and societal changes, they cried. Incarceration of all the bad guys, others replied. Some of them said that all the bad guys had been killed in the crack wars. Ultimately it boiled down to a few profound changes, the most important, in Maple's mind, being accountability! The bosses were being held accountable, and, because the blame always runs downhill, the bosses held the cops accountable. Under previous administrations, arrests were considered to be part of the cost doing business. Unlike summonses, arrests cost the city money, because they usually required cops to work overtime to process the arrests and to go to court for the arraignment. Maple understood this, because he had been on the other side of that coin. Maple knew that arrest overtime would have to go up, as would uniform overtime to patrol the hotspots where crime was happening. But Giuliani was on board this train, at least for a while. The new mayor understood that crime reductions would come at a price, a price he was willing to pay.

Because of Maple's staunch belief in accountability and effective management, there was little room for the precepts and ideas of community policing. Apparently Maple had been watching and observing these strategies during the Ben Ward years and later during Lee Brown's tenure, and did not feel that they were effective. He did not hide his feelings about these quality-of-life initiatives:

> The implication is, if the police would take care of the little things, the big things would take care of themselves.

> How sad. That idea was tested in New York's subways in the late 1980's along with a strain of community policing that encouraged supervisors to be "coaches" instead of leaders. The result was an 87 percent rise in subway robberies from 1987 to the middle of 1990.[10]

Maple did not disguise his contempt for some of his predecessor's strategies but also acknowledged that in some limited situations community policing might complement his Compstat initiatives. But he was quick to point out the problems and shortcomings of community oriented policing, especially as it had been implemented in New York City:

> The community policing officers, an army of baby cops who'd been more or less left on their own to solve all the problems in the city, were to their credit, quick learners. Most all of them decided the best way to address crime and quality-of-life problem on their beats was to work from ten in the morning to six at night, but never on weekends.[11]

Perhaps a harsh rebuke for the centerpiece of Lee Brown's policing strategies, Maple was a cop who had lived through the worst crime period in New York City history, and realized exactly what the problem was. Nobody cared enough to make the profound changes that were necessary to turn the tide against crime. Maple knew that, and it was back to that word accountable again, the bosses of the NYPD had not been held accountable for many, many years, and as a result, crime was allowed to not only proliferate, but to flourish. No, Maple was having none of the feel-good policing initiatives, his strategy demanded accountability and effective management:

> The giveaway that community policing was hatched by academics is how the model devalues the role of supervisors. Everything is left up to the individual cop, including the hours he or she is going to work, which explains why the community policing officers in the old NYPD mostly worked ten to six and took weekends off.[12]

The operative words in that quote are "the old NYPD." In William Bratton's and Jack Maple's new NYPD, the supervisors were in charge and they would be held accountable. In fact, everybody would be held accountable. Indeed, a sea change had occurred. Community policing for the most part was out, and Compstat was in. And Compstat employed all the ideas that Maple talked about as a crime fighter.

The new strategies, the encouragement of arrests, and the accompanying overtime were all morale boosters to the NYPD, at least for a while. The handcuffs had come off and the cops were making arrests and they were making money. And, as arrests went up, crime reports went down. Soon the headlines featured the incredible crime reductions instead of the ubiquitous murder or rape. And then the tourists started coming back to New York City. What did it take? In a word, accountability. A mayor who felt accountable to the electorate as he endeavored to lower crime and create a safer city. A police commissioner who understood the mandate and implemented new strategies; he held his managers accountable, and they responded. Ultimately it was the cops who did the job, a job most of them knew well. All they needed was encouragement, focus, and the support of management.

Political Accountability

What does all of this have to do with Crown Heights? Well, it may not have been possible if not for Crown Heights. It was the Crown Heights Riots in 1991 that became the last straw for David Dinkins' administration. The violence and the fear that the Lubavitchers experienced that fateful week in August was the impetus for that group to change its political affiliation. Of course it wasn't only the Lubavitchers who were affected, and those effects were reflected in the voting booth. The 1993 election was a referendum on David Dinkins with the Jews in Crown Heights and other precincts in the city weighing in. The margin of victory Dinkins enjoyed over Giuliani in 1989 was very close to his margin of defeat in 1993. And that is where Crown Heights enters the picture.

The Lubavitcher rebbe had consistently delivered the votes of Crown Heights to the Democratic Party. Voting in a bloc has great advantages, and the Lubavitchers, as we have seen, used their advantages the way just about any other group would. In the mayoral election of 1989 those votes helped put Dinkins in City Hall as the first black mayor of New York. But the Crown Heights Riot had greatly disillusioned the Lubavitchers and many other Jews throughout the city. The Lubavitchers made no secret of the fact that they felt abandoned by the mayor as thugs and hooligans smashed windows, burned buildings, and wreaked havoc on the neighborhood.

These sentiments were made known in the media. The Jewish press, as well as the mainstream media (including the *New York Times*), carried articles and editorials that said as much. The coalition had finally broken apart, and the telltale would be the NYC mayoral election of 1993. As close as the election was, it became obvious that in 1993 Giuliani would fare much better in Brooklyn and Queens, as Democratic defectors pushed him into City Hall. Many neighborhoods and precincts contributed to his victory. And naturally, one of those areas was Crown Heights.

In the *American Jewish Year Book*, Jerome Chanes explained the political realities in New York City:

> In a sequel to the 1989 mayoral election, in which Dinkins defeated Giuliani by 48,000 votes, Giuliani was the victor in 1993 by 44,000 votes. In a city that is home to some 1.03 million Jews, who comprise 17 percent of the electorate, Jewish voters gave Giuliani 68 percent of their vote, 5 percent more than he received in 1989.[13]

But the defections from the Dinkins camp had far more serious implications for the Democratic Party. A major constituency, one whom the Democratic Machine had consistently counted on, had repudiated that machine and pulled the Republican lever. This was indeed accountability, and it had finally entered the voting booth. The Lubavitchers and Jews from other parts of the city had turned away from the Democratic Party, and took just enough votes to change the course of a city. No one could have known it on that Tuesday night in November 1993, but New York City would not have another Democratic mayor for at least 20 years. Had any political pundit dared utter such heresy, he or she would have been laughed out of the city. But that is what happened.

The astonishing results are explained in the following tables: 1993 and 1989 Election Results: Mayoral New York City:

1993 Election Results

General Election								
		Manhattan	**The Bronx**	**Brooklyn**	**Queens**	**Staten Island**	**Total**
Change in Giuliani margin		+21,433	+8,256	+27,786	+16,428	+26,517	**+100,447**
Giuliani–Dinkins, 1989		–97,600	–72,471	–39,071	+94,670	+67,392	**–47,080**
Giuliani–Dinkins, 1993		–76,167	–64,215	–11,285	+111,098	+93,909	**+53,367**
Republican–Liberal	**Rudolph W. Giuliani**	166,357	98,780	258,058	291,625	115,416	**930,236**

Democratic	**David N. Dinkins**	242,524	162,995	269,343	180,527	21,507	**876,869**
Conservative–Right to Life	**George J. Marlin**						**15,926**
This chart reflects the change in votes for Giuliani. While he still lost Brooklyn and Manhattan, the substantial gains in each borough sealed the victory.							**1,889,003**

1989 Election Results

General Election							
		Manhattan	**The Bronx**	**Brooklyn**	**Queens**	**Staten Island**	**Total**
Dinkins' lead over Giuliani		**+97,600**	**+72,471**	**+39,071**	**–94,670**	**–67,392**	**+47,080**
Democratic	**David N. Dinkins**	255,286	172,271	276,903	190,096	22,988	**917,544**
Republican–Liberal–Independent	**Rudolph W. Giuliani**	157,686	99,800	237,832	284,766	90,380	**870,464**
Right to Life	**Henry Hewes**						**17,460**
Conservative	**Ronald S. Lauder**						**9,271**
Dinkins carried three of the five boroughs by a commanding measure in 1989. Things changed dramatically in 1993.							**1,899,845**

It is ironic to note that it was not necessarily the abominable crime stats that were the undoing of Dinkins and the Democrats, although certainly those issues had a deleterious effect. It was the fact that a devoted and loyal voting base felt abandoned and decided to hold that politician accountable. Twenty-five years of rising crime and a deteriorating quality of life apparently did not have the effect that four days of riot and mayhem did. That riot opened many eyes. Not only in Crown Heights, but across New York City.

Chanes analyzed the divergent ideology and demographics within an ethnic/religious constituency:

Analysts of New York City political affairs noted that Dinkins took office in 1990 with significant approval ratings among Jews. These positive feelings did not last, among other reasons because of allegations that the Dinkins administration favored African-Americans, as well as a perceived decline in the city's quality of life. Although some attributed his loss of Jewish support to the 1991 Crown Heights riots, exit polls did not show this to be much of a factor. Observers suggested that class and ideological differences among New York's Jews were far more significant: Jews living in the outer boroughs of Brooklyn, Queens, the Bronx, and Staten Island—consisting of working- and middle-class neighborhoods—were concerned about "quality-of-life" issues, and thus leaned toward Giuliani, who promised to be tough on crime; Jewish Manhattan residents, mostly liberal and many of them affluent, were more likely to vote ideologically and thus maintained their Democratic loyalties.[14]

For years, political observers had predicted a "long hot summer" for New York City. When it happened in Crown Heights not that many people were surprised. The cops, the politicians, and the residents knew it was a powder keg waiting to explode. That car accident, the murder of Yankel Rosenbaum, and the four days of riots turned out to be a flashpoint in a melting pot. It was a dangerous and frightening time in Brooklyn and in New York City. But, ironically, those events turned out to be a watershed moment for New York City, because the government was finally seen as unresponsive and incompetent. It took a long time, but the people of New York City came to their senses and voted out the machine that had mismanaged the city for decades. Perhaps it was a political reality borne of desperation, or maybe just anger, but the result of the Crown Heights Riot changed the course of history for the people of New York City.

ENDNOTES

CHAPTER 2 BROOKLYN: THE CITY OF CHURCHES; THE BOROUGH OF STRUGGLE

1. Isaacs, Miriam Gottdank. "Crossing Eastern Parkway in Search of Yiddishkayt," *Jews of Brooklyn*, ed. Ilana Abramovitch and Sean Galvin (Waltham, MA: Brandeis University Press, 1999), 154.
2. Johnson, Jesse. *Against Consolidation. Should Brooklyn Be Annexed to New York?* (Brooklyn, NY: League of Loyal Citizens, 1895?) 9. This original document bears no publishing or copyright date but is believed to be written by Johnson and to have been read to the Oxford Club on January 14, 1885. It may have been published later that year although there are some indications in the document that the publication may have been as late as 1895.
3. VanDerzee, Charlene Claye. *An Introduction to the Black Contribution to the Development of Brooklyn: A Permanent Exhibition* (Brooklyn, NY: New Muse Community Museum of Brooklyn, 1977).
4. Stiles, Henry R. *The Civil, Political, Professional and Ecclesiastical History and Commercial and Industrial Record of the County of Kings and the City of Brooklyn, N.Y. From 1683 to 1884* (New York: W. W. Munsell & Co., 1884) 10.
5. Ibid., 46.
6. McManus, Edgar J. *A History of Negro Slavery in New York* (Syracuse, NY: Syracuse University Press, 1966).
7. Vanderbilt, Gertrude Lefferts. *The Social History of Flatbush and the Manners and Customs of the Dutch Settlers in King's County* (New York: D. Appleton and Company, 1882) 199.
8. "The Brooklyn Eagle," *Crow Hill and Some of Its Suggestions*, December 9, 1988.
9. Manbeck, John B., ed., *The Neighborhoods of Brooklyn* (New Haven, CT: Yale University Press, 1998) 79.
10. Ibid., 79.
11. Connolly, Harold X. *A Ghetto Grows in Brooklyn* (New York: New York University Press, 1977) 7.
12. Wilder, Craig Steven. *A Covenant with Color: Race and Social Power in Brooklyn* (New York: Columbia University Press, 1993).

CHAPTER 3 | BLACKS AND JEWS COME TO BROOKLYN

1. Wilder, Craig Steven. *A Covenant with Color: Race and Social Power in Brooklyn* (New York: Columbia University Press, 1993) 63.
2. Ford, F. Donnie. *Caribbean Americans in New York City* (New York: Arcadia Publishing, 2002) 22.
3. Frommer, Harvey. "The Day the Bums Left Home," *New Brooklyn*, (Summer 1982).
4. Wilder, 212.
5. Ford, 7.
6. Wilder, 65.
7. Rosenthal, Mel, and Roberta Perry-Mapp. "Carnival in Brooklyn: West Indian Day Parade," Exhibitions @ The Brooklyn Public Library Research Website, New York (2004).
8. Burrows, Edwin G., and Mike Wallace. *Gotham: A History of New York City to 1898* (New York: Oxford University Press, 1999) 897.
9. Wilder, 212.
10. Mintz, Jerome R. *Hasidic People* (Cambridge, MA: Harvard University Press, Cambridge, 1992) 104.
11. Ibid.
12. Buber, Martin. *Tales of Hasidim* (New York: Shocken Books, 1991) 41, 266.
13. Harris, Lis. *Holy Days: The World of a Hasidic Family* (New York: Summit Books, 1985) 32.
14. Ibid., 32.
15. Dubnow, Simon. *The History of the Jews in Russia and Poland* (Philadelphia: Avotaynu, 2000).
16. Harris, 40.
17. Harris, 39.
18. Rabinowicz, Harry. *The World of Hasidism* (London: Vallentine Mitchell, 1994) 15.
19. Ibid., 13.
20. Ibid., 29.
21. Hoffman, Edward. *Despite All Odds: The Story of Lubavitch* (New York: Simon & Schuster, 1991) 19.

CHAPTER 4 | A CHANGING COMMUNITY

1. Raab, Selwyn. *The New York Times*, June 23, 1978; Daughtry, Herbert. *No Monopoly on Suffering* (Lawrenceville, NJ: Africa World Press, 1997) 59.

2. Frommer, Harvey. "The Day the Bums Left Home," *New Brooklyn*, (Summer 1982): 9.

3. Wilder, 212.

4. Naison, Mark. "Crown Heights in the 1950's," *Jews of Brooklyn*, edited by Ilana Abramovitch and Sean Galvin (Waltham, MA: Brandeis University Press, 2002) 144.

5. Harris, Lis. *Holy Days: The World of a Hasidic Family* (New York: Summit Books, 1985) 87.

6. Mintz, Jerome R. *Hasidic People* (Cambridge, MA: Harvard University Press, Cambridge, 1992) 144.

7. Mintz, 141.

8. This theme was repeated often throughout the 30-year history of tumult in the Crown Heights neighborhood. The Daughtry quote at the head of the chapter spells out the Reverend's own views of the problem, but this came 14 years after the Macabees' inception.

9. Conason, Joe. *The Village Voice*, July 3, 1978.

10. Mintz, 141.

11. Sanchez, Toby. *The Crown Heights Neighborhood Profile* (New York: Brooklyn In Touch Information Center Inc., 1990) 5.

12. Ibid., 14.

Chapter 5 A City in Decline: Wagner, Lindsay, Beame, and Koch

1. Clarity, James F. "Robert Wagner, 80, Pivotal New York Mayor," *The New York Times*, February 13, 1991.

2. Ibid.

3. Glazer, Nathan, and Daniel Patrick Moynihan. *Beyond the Melting Pot: Race and Ethnicity in New York City* (Cambridge, MA: MIT Press, 1963, 1970), 5.

4. Ibid., xix.

5. Ibid., xii.

6. Weisman, Steven. "How New York Became a Fiscal Junkie," *The New York Times*, August 17, 1975, 191.

7. Bennet, Charles G. *The New York Times*, July 20, 1965.

8. Witkin, Richard. *The New York Times*, October 19, 1965.

9. Newfield, Jack, and Wayne Barrett, *City for Sale: Ed Koch and the Betrayal of New York* (New York: Harper and Row, 1988) 124.

10. Hentoff, Nat. *A Political Life: The Education of John V. Lindsay* (New York: Albert A. Knopf, 1969) 78.

11. *The New York Daily News*, November 1, 1975.

12. Barrett, Wayne, and Jack Newfield. *Abuse of Power: The Permanent Governor and the Fall of New York* (New York: Viking Press, 1977) 45.
13. Ibid., 171.
14. Barrett and Newfield, 132–35.

CHAPTER 6 | WELCOME BACK TO THE CLUBHOUSE

1. McNickle, Chris. *To Be Mayor of New York: Ethnic Politics in the City* (New York: Columbia University Press, 1993) 7–9.
2. Barrett, Wayne, and Jack Newfield. *Abuse of Power: The Permanent Governor and the Fall of New York* (New York: Viking Press, 1977) 114.
3. Daughtry, Herbert. *No Monopoly on Suffering* (Lawrenceville, NJ: Africa World Press, 1993) 48–50.
4. Price, Eric. *The New York Times*, December 9, 1989.
5. Lichtenstein, Grace. "Madison Democratic Club Brings Influence to Brooklyn," *The New York Times*, November 8, 1974.
6. Ibid.
7. DeSena, Judith N. *People Power: Grass Roots Politics and Race Relations* (New York: University Press of America, Inc., 1999) 25.
8. Barrett and Newfield, 438. Actually, the entire book pushes the premise that Koch's entire administration was ambivalent about corruption throughout the 12-year reign and makes numerous cases for this argument, including the Parking Violations scandal and the suicide of Donald Manes.
9. Ibid., 137.
10. Ibid., 132.
11. Daughtry, 191.

CHAPTER 7 | THE POLITICS OF CONFRONTATION

1. Abibdika, Mwlina (Robert Sonny Carson). *The Education of Sonny Carson* (New York: W. W. Norton and Co., 1972).
2. Daughtry, *No Monopoly on Suffering* (Lawrenceville, NJ: Africa World Press, 1997) 25.
3. Conason, Joe. *The Village Voice*, July 3, 1978.
4. Daughtry. P.27
5. Mintz, Jerome R. *Hasidic People* (Cambridge, MA: Harvard University Press, 1992) 103.

6. Daughtry, Herbert. *Inside the Storm: My Role in Crown Heights*, 32.

7. Daughtry, 27.

8. Sanchez, 16.

9. Ibid., 25.

10. Ibid., 17.

CHAPTER 8 | THE DAYS OF OUTRAGE

1. Noel, Peter, and Charles Baillou. *The Amsterdam News*, April 18, 1987.

2. Abibdika, Mwlina (Robert Sonny Carson). *The Education of Sonny Carson* (New York: W. W. Norton and Co., 1972) 53.

3. Geltman, Max. *The Confrontation: Black Power, Anti-Semitism, and the Myth of Integration* (Englewood Cliffs: Prentice Hall, Inc., 1970) 69. In *The Confrontation*, Geltman postulates the etymology of the word ghetto is from the Italian word for foundry which was an area in the old city of Venice where the Jews were forced to live in a walled city in 1516.

4. Abibdika, 54.

5. Ibid., 108.

6. Ibid., 103.

7. McNickle, Chris. *To Be Mayor of New York: Ethnic Politics in the City* (New York: Columbia University Press, 1993) 218.

8. Dollinger, Marc. "A Different Kind of Freedom Ride: American Jews and the Struggle for Racial Equality 1964–1975," *An Inventory of Promises: Essays on American Jewish History in Honor of Moses Rischin,* ed. Jeffrey Gurrock and Marc Lee Raphael. (Brooklyn, NY: Carlson Publishing Inc., 1995) 62.

9. Ibid.

10. Geltman, 181.

11. Abibdika, 195.

12. Purham, Todd S. "Ward Discloses a Secret Inquiry on Black Group," *The New York Times*, July, 17, 1987. The "monitoring" of the New York 8 would be a sore point in the NYPD for many years following the revelation and acknowledgment by an embarrassed commissioner Ward that there was indeed a "Black Desk" in the NYPD Intelligence Division. Following that startling revelation Ward also informed the media that it was a "stupid" idea and that subunit would be disbanded.

13. De Santis, John. *Yusuf Hawkins: For the Color of His Skin* (Cambridge, MA: Harvard University Press, 1991) 8.

14. McFadden, Robert D. "Day of Outrage March Ends in Violence," *The New York Times*, September 2, 1989.

15. Ibid.

16. From the *Papers of Mayor David N. Dinkins* Box #2 Accn #94-40, Memo from Deputy Mayor Bill Lynch.

17. Ibid., from the Committee on General Welfare's examination of the "Report of the Mayor's Committee Investigating the Protest Against Two Korean-Owned Groceries on Church Avenue in Brooklyn" 2.

18. Ibid., 7.

19. "Anti-Semitism Among Black Student Groups," Jewish Virtual Library (Website).

20. The Nation of Islam Historical Research Department. *The Secret Relationship Between Blacks and Jews* (Boston: Lattimer Associates, 1991).

21. Ibid., vii.

22. Dollinger, 64.

23. Faber, Eli. *Jews, Slaves and the Slave Trade: Setting the Record Straight* (New York: New York University Press, 1998).

24. Ibid., 8.

25. Ibid., 15.

26. Ibid., 12, 19.

27. Lubasch, Arnold, "'A Rehearsal for a Stickup' Is Linked to Brink's," *The New York Times*, July 1985.

28. Singh, Robert. *The Farrakhan Phenomenon: Race, Reaction, and the Paranoid Style in American Politics* (Washington, DC: Georgetown University Press, 1997) 86.

29. Manning, Marable. *Black Leadership* (New York: Columbia University Press, 1998) 172.

30. King, Martin Luther, Jr. *Why We Can't Wait* (New York: Harper & Row, Publishers, 1963) 59.

31. Ibid., 132.

32. Ibid., 4.

33. Ibid., 136.

34. Geltman, 181.

35. Ibid., 182.

36. Abibdika, 147.

37. Singh, 43.

CHAPTER 9 | RAY POWERS

1. De Santis, John. *For the Color of His Skin: The Murder of Yusuf Hawkins and the Trial of Bensonhurst* (New Delhi: Pharos Books, 1991) 76.
2. Lubasch, Arnold. "Conspiracy Defendants Characterized as Activists," *The New York Times*, June 27, 1985; "Second New York 8 Member Held in Orange County," *The New York Times*, July 19, 1987.
3. Girgenti, Richard. *A Report to the Governor on the Disturbances in Crown Heights: An Assessment of the City's Preparedness and Response to Civil Disorder* (Albany, NY: New York State Division of Criminal Justice Services, 1993) 87.
4. Ibid., 75.
5. Ibid., 95.
6. Ibid., 83. The Girgenti Commission reported just such a situation in which a mob of rioters had succeeded in breaking a door off its hinges. The only thing that held it on was the dead-bolt.
7. Ibid., 83.
8. Rosenthal, A. M. "POGROM in BROOKLYN," *The New York Times*, September 3, 1991.
9. Rosenthal, A. M."Burning the Bridges: Strategy of the Hate Business," *The New York Times*, September 6, 1991.
10. Rosenthal, A. M. September 3, 1991.
11. Boyd, Herb *Amsterdam News.*
12. Girgenti, 359.
13. Ibid., 359.
14. Ibid., 360.
15. Van Gelder, Lawrence *The New York Times*, March 7, 1995.
16. Klein, Woody. *Lindsay's Promise: The Dream That Failed; A Personal Account by Woody Klein.* (New York: MacMillan Co., 1970) 64.
17. The interviewee requested anonymity.

CHAPTER 10 | THE RIOT: AS AMERICAN AS APPLE PIE

1. Headley, T. J. *Great Riots of New York 1712–1893* (New York: E. B. Treat & Co., 1913) 27.
2. Ibid., 17.
3. Ibid., 28.

4. Rubenstein, Richard, and Robert M. Fogelson, eds. *Story of the Riot Published by the Citizens Protective League* (New York: Arno Press Inc. and *The New York Times*, 1969) 1.

Chapter 11 A Hungry Mob Is an Angry Mob

1. Marley, Bob. "Natty Dread," Def Jam Records (1976).
2. Daughtry, Herbert. *No Monopoly on Suffering* (Lawrenceville, NJ: Africa World Press, 1997) 49.
3. James Barron, "Two Deaths Ignite Racial Clash in Tense Brooklyn Neighborhood," *The New York Times*, August 21, 1991.
4. John T. McQuiston, "Fatal Crash Starts Melee with Police in Brooklyn," *The New York Times*, August 20, 1991.
5. John Kifner, "Police Battle Familiar Charges of Favoritism Toward Hasidim," *The New York Times*, August 21, 1991.
6. Girgenti, Richard. *A Report to the Governor on the Disturbances in Crown Heights: An Assessment of the City's Preparedness and Response to Civil Disorder* (Albany, NY: New York State Division of Criminal Justice Services, 1993) 56
7. *The New York Times*, August 23, 1992.
8. Girgenti, 64.
9. J.J. Goldberg, *The New York Times*, September 1, 1993, 19.
10. Seth Faison Jr. "Police Official Is Critical of Lack of Preparation," *The New York Times*, August 24, 1991.
11. Ibid.
12. Goldberg
13. Rosenthal, A. M."Burning the Bridges: Strategy of the Hate Business," *The New York Times*, September 6, 1991.
14. Dennis Hevesi, "Pogrom and Stereotypes, Crown Heights Is No Blend," *The New York Times*, August 21, 1991.
15. Kelly would later be named police commissioner in 1994 by Mayor Rudy Giuliani and would again return as commissioner under Mayor Michael Bloomberg.
16. Girgenti, 95.
17. Ibid., 97.
18. Ibid., 105.
19. Mintz, Jerome R. *Hasidic People* (Cambridge, MA: Harvard University Press, Cambridge, 1992) 336.
20. Ibid., 336.

21. Rosenthal, Sept. 3, 1991; Hevesi on August 21,1991

22. Girgenti, 346.

23. Girgenti, 363.

24. Girgenti, 359.

25. Dinkins Statement from Girgenti, 6.

26. Ibid., 18.

CHAPTER 12 | THE MEDIA RETURNS A VERDICT

1. Lee, Felicia. "Bitterness Pervades Funeral," *The New York Times*, August 27, 1991.
2. Ibid.
3. Goldman, Ari. "Who's in Control?" *The New York Times*, August 25, 1991
4. Gourevitch, Philip. "The Crown Heights Riot and its Aftermath," *The Jewish Daily Forward*, January 1993.
5. Daughtry, Herbert. *No Monopoly on Suffering* (Lawrenceville, NJ: Africa World Press, 1997).
6. Daughtry, Herbert. *Inside the Storm: My Role in Crown Heights*. (New York, N.Y. H. Daughtry publisher, New York 1991)
7. Ibid.

CHAPTER 13 | POLICING IN NEW YORK CITY: THE HANDCUFFS COME OFF

1. Haring, Sidney, and Gerda W. Ray. "Policing a Class Society: New York City in the 1990's," *The Experience of American Cities*, 26 Soc. Just.63 1999).
2. Geltman, *The Confrontation: Black Power, Anti-Semitism, and the Myth of Integration* (Englewood Cliffs: Prentice Hall, Inc., 1970) 39.
3. Jacoby, Tamar. *CityJournal.org*, January 1993.
4. *The New York Times*, April 2, 1995.
5. Maas, Peter. *Serpico* (New York: Harper Collins 1973).
6. Knapp Commission, United States Commission on Civil Rights, usccr.gov/pubs/guard.
7. Newburn, Tim. "Understanding and Preventing Police Corruption," *Home Office: Research Development and Statistics*, www.homeoffice.gov.uk.
8. "Analysis of Police Corruption," *Cyberessays.org*, 1998.

9. Ibid.

10. "Police Brutality and Accountability in the U.S.," *Shielded from Justice, Human Rights Watch*, 1998, www.hrw.org/reports98.

11. *New York Times*, April 2. 1995.

12. Pritchett, Wendell E. *From One Ghetto to Another: Blacks, Jews and Public Housing in Brownsville, Brooklyn 1945–1970*, A Dissertation in History (Philadelphia: University of Pennsylvania, 1997).

13. Jacoby, 1.

14. *Migration News, UC Davis*, migrationucdavis.edu/mn.

15. *The Village Voice*, August 27, 1988.

16. Horowitz, Craig. "Brooklyn Burning," *New York Magazine*, April 7, 2003, 19.

17. Ibid.

18. Siegel, Fred. "The Crown Heights Pogrom," Character.com, January 18, 2006.

19. Bratton, William J., and William Andrews. "Crime and Punishment: What We've Learned about Policing," *City Journal*, Spring (1999).

    a.Bratton, William and Andrews "Crime and Punishment: What We've Learned about Policing,"

20. Krauss, Clifford. "Drop in Crime," *The New York Times*, July 19, 1995.

CHAPTER 14 | NOBODY OWNS A NEIGHBORHOOD:

1. Interview with retired NYPD captain Joseph Murphy, who related that this was a direct command from commissioner Brown during his initial meeting with upper level commanders early in Brown's new administration.

2. Purnick, Joyce. "Metro Matters," *The New York Times*, May 8, 1995.

CHAPTER 15 | THE POLICE AND THE COMMUNITY

1. Bratton, William J., and William Andrews. "Crime and Punishment: What We've Learned About Policing," *City Journal*, Spring (1999).

2. Goldstein, Herman. *The New Policing: Confronting Complexity* (Washington, DC: National Institute of Justice, December 1993).

3. FBI Unified Crime Reports for 1988 through 1994.

4. Wolf, Craig. *The New York Times*, August 4, 1992.

5. Ibid.

6. Maple, John, and Christopher Mitchell. *The Crime Fighter* (New York: Broadway Books, 1999) 8.

7. Ibid.

8. Ibid.

9. Ibid.

10. Ibid., 35.Ibid.

11.

12. Ibid.

13. Chanes, Jerome A., *American Jewish Year Book*, 95(11995): 101–28, 1995.

14. Ibid., 128.

BIBLIOGRAPHY

Abubdika, Mwlina. *The Education of Sonny Carson.* New York: W.W. Norton and Co., 1972.

Allen, Theodore. *The Invention of the White Race.* London-New York: Verso Books, 1994.

"Analysis of Police Corruption." *Cyberessays.org*, 1998. Retrieved March 2006 from www.cyberessays.org.

"Anti-Semitism Among Black Student Groups." *The Jewish Virtual Library.* Retrieved March 2006 from www.jewishvirtuallibrary.org.

Barrett, Wayne, and Jack Newfield. *City for Sale: Ed Koch and the Betrayal of New York.* New York: Harper & Row, 1988.

———. *Abuse of Power: The Permanent Governor and the Fall of New York.* New York: Viking Press, 1977.

Barron, James. "Two Deaths Ignite Racial Clash in Tense Brooklyn Neighborhood," *The New York Times*, August 21, 1991.

Bennet, Charles G. *The New York Times*, July 20, 1965.

Bennet, Lerone, Jr. *The Negro Mood and Other Essays.* Chicago: Johnson Publishing Co. Inc., 1964.

———. *Before the Mayflower: A History of Black America.* New York: Penguin Books, 1962.

Berger, David, ed. *The Legacy of Jewish Immigration: 1881 and Its Impact.* New York: Brooklyn College Press, 1983.

Breitman, George. *The Last Year of Malcolm X: The Evolution of a Revolutionary.* New York: Pathfinder, 1967.

Brereton, Bridget. *Society and Culture in the Caribbean, The Modern Caribbean.* London and Chapel Hill, NC: The University of North Carolina Press, 1989.

Bridges, George Wilson. *The Annals of Jamaica.* London: Frank Cass & Co. Ltd., 1828.

Buber, Martin. *Tales of Hasidim.* New York: Shocken Books, 1991.

Building Commission of Kings County. *Report of the Buildings Committee in Manner of Erection and Furnishing of the Court House.* Brooklyn: Union Steam Presses, 1865.

Clarity, James F. "Robert Wagner, 80, Pivotal New York Mayor," *The New York Times*, February 13, 1991.

Cundall, Frank. *Biographical Annals of Jamaica.* Kingston: Institute of Jamaica by the Educational Supply Co., 1904.

Conason, Joe. *The Village Voice*, July 3, 1978.

Connolly, Harold X. *A Ghetto Grows in Brooklyn*. New York: New York University Press, 1977.

———. "Bedford Stuyvesant," in *An Introduction to the Black Contribution to the Development of Brooklyn: A Permanent Exhibition*, edited by Charlene Claye VanDerzee. New York: New Muse Community Museum of Brooklyn, 1977.

"Crow Hill and Some of Its Suggestions," *The Brooklyn Eagle*, December 9, 1888.

Daughtry, Herbert. *Inside the Storm: My Role in Crown Heights*. Lawrenceville, NJ: Africa World Press, 1992.

———. *No Monopoly on Suffering*. Lawrenceville, NJ: Africa World Press, 1993.

Davis, H. P. *Black Democracy: The Story of Haiti* (3rd ed.). New York: Biblo and Tannen, 1967.

De Santis, John. *Yusuf Hawkins: For the Color of His Skin*. Cambridge, MA: Harvard University Press, 1991.

———. *For the Color of His Skin: The Murder of Yusuf Hawkins and the Trial of Bensonhurst*. New Delhi: Pharos Books 1991.

DeSena, Judith N. *People Power: Grass Roots Politics and Race Relations*. New York: University Press of America, Inc., 1999.

Dollinger, Marc. "A Different Kind of Freedom Ride: American Jews and the Struggle for Racial Equality 1964–1975," in *An Inventory of Promises: Essays on American Jewish History in Honor of Moses Rischin*, edited by Jeffrey Gurrock and Marc Lee Raphael. Brooklyn, New York: Carlson Publishing Inc., 1995.

Dotterer, Ronald, Deborah Dash Moore, and Steven Cohen. *Jewish Settlement and Community in the Modern Western World*. London: Susquehanna University Press, 1991.

Drummonds, Mario. "Slavery in Brooklyn," in *An Introduction to the Black Contribution to the Development of Brooklyn: A Permanent Exhibition*, edited by Charlene Claye VanDerzee. Brooklyn: New Muse Community Museum of Brooklyn, 1977.

Dubnow, Simon. *The History of the Jews in Russia and Poland*. Philadelphia: Avotaynu, 2000.

DuBois, W. E. B. *The Souls of Black Folk*. New York: W. W. Norton & Company, 1903.

Faber, Eli. *Jews, Slaves and the Slave Trade: Setting the Record Straight*. New York: New York University Press, 1998.

Faison, Seth, Jr. "Police Official Is Critical of Lack of Preparation," *The New York Times*, August 24, 1991.

Ford, F. Donnie. *Caribbean Americans in New York City*. New York: Arcadia Publishing, 2002.

Frommer, Harvey. "The Day the Bums Left Home," *New Brooklyn*, Summer (1982).

Galenson, David W. *Traders, Planters, and Slaves: Market Behaviour in Early English America*. London: Cambridge University Press, 1986.

Gardner, W. J. *History of Jamaica from Its Discovery by Christopher Columbus to the Year 1872*. Oxford: Frank Cass and Co., 1971.

Geltman, Max. *The Confrontation: Black Power, Anti-Semitism, and the Myth of Integration.* Englewood Cliffs: NJ: Prentice Hall Inc., 1970.

Gershon, David Hundert. *New Perspectives on Hasidism.* New York: Hunter College Jewish Social Studies Program Thought #17: New York, 2002

Girgenti, Richard H. *A Report to the Governor on the Disturbances in Crown Heights: A Review of the Investigation into the Death of Yankel Rosenbaum and the Resulting Prosecution.* Albany, NY: New York State of Criminal Justice, 1993.

———. *A Report to the Governor on the Disturbances in Crown Heights, Vol.1: An Assessment of the City's Preparedness and Response to Civil Disorder.* Albany, NY: New York State Division of Criminal Justice, 1993.

Glazer, Nathan, and Daniel Patrick Moynihan. *Beyond the Melting Pot.* Cambridge, MA: MIT Press, 1963 and 1970.

Goldberg, J. J. *The New York Times*, September 1, 1993.

Goldman, Ari. "Who's in Control?" *The New York Times*, August 25, 1991.

Gourevitch, Philip. "The Crown Heights Riot and Its Aftermath," *The Jewish Daily Forward*, January 1993.

Groh, George. *The Black Migration: The Journey to Urban America.* New York: Weybright and Talley, 1972.

Gurock, Jeffrey S., and Marc Lee Raphael, eds. *An Inventory of Promises: Essays on American Jewish History in Honor of Moses Rischin.* Brooklyn, New York: Carlson Publishing, 1995.

Handlin, Oscar. *The Newcomers.* Cambridge, MA: Harvard University Press, 1959.

———. *Race and Nationality in American Life.* Boston:.Little Brown and Co., 1957.

Haring, Sidney, and Gerda W. Ray. *Policing a Class Society: New York City in the 1990's.* New York: Social Justice Summer, 1999.

Harris, Lis. *Holy Days: The World of a Hasidic Family.* New York: Summit Books, 1985.

Headley, J. T. *Great Riots of New York 1712–1873.* New York: E. B. Treat, 1891.

Hentoff, Nat. *A Political Life: The Education of John V. Lindsay.* New York: Albert A. Knopf, 1969.

Herskovits, Melville J. *The New Negro World: Selected Papers in Afroamerican Studies.* Indianapolis, IN: Indiana University Press, 1966.

Hertzberg, Arthur. *A Jew in America.* San Francisco: Harper 2002.

Hevesi, Dennis. "Pogrom and Stereotypes, Crown Heights Is No Blend," *The New York Times*, August 21, 1991.

Hoffman, Edward. *Despite All Odds: The Story of Lubavitch.* New York: Simon and Schuster, 1991.

Holt, Thomas C., and Elsa Barkley Brown, eds. *Major Problems in African-American History Vol.1 From Slavery to Freedom, 1619–1877.* Boston and New York: Houghton Mifflin Co., 2000.

Horowitz, Craig. "Brooklyn Burning," *New York Magazine*, April 7, 2003.

Howe, Irving. *World of Our Fathers.* New York: Harcourt Brace Jovanovich, 1976.

Isaacs, Miriam Gottdank. "Crossing Eastern Parkway in Search of Yiddishkayt," in *Jews of Brooklyn*, edited by Ilana Abramovitch and Sean Galvin. Waltham, MA: Brandeis University Press, 1999.

Jacoby, Tamar. *CityJournal.org.* January 1993. Retrieved March 2006 from www.cityjournal.org.

Johnson, Jesse. *Against Consolidation. Should Brooklyn Be Annexed to New York?* Brooklyn, NY: League of Loyal Citizens, 1895.

Kifner, John. "Police Battle Familiar Charges of Favoritism Toward Hasidim," *The New York Times*, August 21, 1991.

King, Martin Luther, Jr. *Why We Can't Wait.* New York: Harper & Row, 1963.

Klein, Woody. *Lindsay's Promise: The Dream That Failed; A Personal Account by Woody Klein.* New York: The MacMillan Co., 1970.

Knapp Commission. *United States Commission on Civil Rights.* Retrieved March 2006 from usccr.gov/pubs/guard.

Knight, Frank W., and Colin A. Palmer, eds. *The Modern Caribbean.* London and Chapel Hill, NC: The University of North Carolina Press, 1989.

Krauss, Clifford. "Drop in Crime," *The New York Times*, July 19, 1995.

Lee, Felicia. "Bitterness Pervades Funeral," *The New York Times*, August 27, 1991.

Levine, Stephanie Wellen. *Mystics, Mavericks, and Merrymakers: An Intimate Journey Among Hasidic Girls.* New York: New York University Press, 2003.

Libo, Kenneth, and Irving Howe. *We Lived There Too.* New York: St. Martin's/Marek, 1984.

Lichtenstein, Grace. "Madison Democratic Club Brings Influence to Brooklyn," *The New York Times*, November 8, 1974.

Lubasch, Arnold. "Conspiracy Defendants Characterized as Activists," *The New York Times*, June 27, 1985.

———. "A Rehearsal for a Stickup Is Linked to Brink's," *The New York Times*, July 1985.

——— "Second New York 8 Member Held in Orange County," *The New York Times*, July 19, 1987.

Lynch, Bill. *Memo to Mayor David N. Dinkins: Report of the Mayor's Committee Investigating the Protest Against Two Korean-Owned Groceries on Church Avenue in Brooklyn.* Papers of Mayor David N. Dinkins Box #2, Accn #94-40. New York: New York City Municipal Archives, 1990.

The Nation of Islam Historical Research Department. *The Secret Relationship Between Blacks and Jews.* Boston: Lattimer Associates, 1991.

Maas, Peter. *Serpico.* New York: Harper Collins, 1973.

Manbeck, John B., ed. *The Neighborhoods of Brooklyn.* New Haven, CT: Yale University Press, 1998.

Manning, Marable. *Black Leadership.* New York: Columbia University Press, 1998.

Marley, Bob. "Natty Dread." Def Jam Records, 1976.

Maynard, Joan, and Gwen Cottman. *Weeksville: Then and Now.* New York: The Society for the Preservation of Weeksville and Bedford Stuyvesant History, 1983.

McFadden, Robert D. "Day of Outrage March Ends in Violence," *The New York Times*, September 2, 1989.

McManus, Edgar J. *A History of Negro Slavery in New York.* New York: Syracuse University Press, 1966.

McNickle, Chris. *To Be Mayor of New York: Ethnic Politics in the City.* New York: Columbia University Press, 1993.

McQuiston, John T. "Fatal Crash Starts Melee with Police in Brooklyn," *The New York Times*, August 20, 1991.

Migration News, UC Davis. Retrieved March 2006 from migrationucdavis.edu/mn.

Mintz, Jerome R. *Hasidic People: A Place in the New World.* Cambridge, MA: Harvard University Press, 1992.

Mollenkopf, John Hull. *A Phoenix in the Ashes: The Rise and Fall of the Koch Coalition in New York City Politics.* Princeton, NJ: Princeton University Press, 1992.

Moore, Deborah Dash. *At Home in America: Second Generation New York Jews.* New York: Columbia University Press, 1981.

Morgan, Kenneth. *Slavery and Servitude in Colonial North America: A Short History.* New York: New York University Press, 2001.

Murphy, Joseph. Interview by Brendan Finn. January 2004.

Naison, Mark. *Crown Heights in the 1950's. Jews of Brooklyn.* Edited by Ilana Abramovitch and Sean Galvin. Waltham, MA: Brandeis University Press, 2002.

The New York Daily News, November 1, 1975.

New York State Historical Association. *Proceedings of the Seventh Annual Meeting of the New York State Historical Association, held August 22nd, 1905, at the Court House, Lake George, New York.* New York: New York State Historical Association, 1905.

The New York Times, April 2, 1995.

Newburn, Tim. "Understanding and Preventing Police Corruption." *Home Office; Research Development and Statistics.* Retrieved March 2006 from www.homeoffice.gov.uk.

Noel, Peter, and Charles Baillou, *The Amsterdam News*, April 18, 1987.

O'Callaghan, E. B. *Voyages of the Slavers St. John and Arms of Amsterdam 1659, 1663; Together with Additional Papers illustrative of the Slave Trade under the Dutch.* Albany, NY: J. Munsell, 1867.

Ostrander, Stephen M. *History of the City of Brooklyn and Kings County.* Brooklyn, NY: Subscription Brooklyn, 1894.

"Police Brutality and Accountability in the U.S." *Shielded from Justice, Human Rights Watch,* 1998. Retrieved March 2006 from www.hrw.org/reports98.

Price, Eric. *The New York Times*, December 9, 1989.

Pritchett, Wendell. *From One Ghetto to Another: Blacks, Jews and Public Housing in Brownsville, Brooklyn, 1945–1976, A Dissertation in History.* Philadelphia: University of Pennsylvania, 1997.

Purham, Todd S. "Ward Discloses a Secret Inquiry on Black Group," *The New York Times*, July 17, 1987.

Purnick, Joyce. "Metro Matters," *The New York Times*, May 8, 1995.

Quarles, Benjamin. *The Negro in the Making of America.* New York: Simon & Schuster, 1964.

Raab, Selwyn. *The New York Times*, June 23, 1978.

Rabinowicz, Harold. *The World of Hasidism.* London: Vallentine-Mitchell, 1994.

Raphael, Mare Lee, ed. *"Jewishness" And the World of "Difference" in the United States.* Williamsburg, VA: William and Mary College Department of Religion, 2001.

Raynal, Abbe. *Philosophical and Political History of the Settlement and Trade of the Europeans in the East and West Indies.* Translated by J. Justamond. London: Printed for T. Caddel in the Strand, 1777.

Richardson, Bonham C. *Caribbean Migrations, from The Modern Caribbean.* London and Chapel Hill, NC: The University of North Carolina Press, 1989.

Roche, Spencer. *A Discourse Delivered in St. Mark's Church, Brooklyn on Sunday, November Fifteenth, 1885 by Reverend Spencer Roche.* Brooklyn, NY: Orphans Press, 1885.

Rosenthal, A. M. "POGROM in BROOKLYN," *The New York Times*, September 3, 1991.

———. "Burning the Bridges: Strategy of the Hate Business," *The New York Times*, September 6, 1991.

Rosenthal, Mel, and Roberta Perry-Mapp, "Carnival in Brooklyn: West Indian Day Parade," *The Brooklyn Public Library Research Website; Exhibitions.* New York, 2004. Retrieved March 2006. From *www.brooklynpubliclibrary.org/.../exhibitions/carnival-brooklyn.*

Royal Adventurers of England Trading into Africa. *Answer of the Company of Royal Adventurers of England Trading into Africa.* England: Royal Adventurers of England Trading into Africa, 1667.

Rubenstein, Richard, and Robert M. Fogelson. "Story of the Riot. New York: Citizens Protective League," *New York Times*, 1969.

Sanchez, Toby. *The Crown Heights Neighborhood Profile.* New York: Brooklyn In Touch Information Center Inc., 1990.

Siegel, Fred. "The Crown Heights Pogrom." *InCharacter.com.* January 18, 2006. Retrieved March 2006 from incharacter.com.

Singh, Robert. *The Farrakhan Phenomenon: Race, Reaction and the Paranoid Style in American Politics.* Washington, DC: Georgetown University Press, 1997.

Sorin, Gerald. *The Nurturing Neighborhood: The Brownsville Boys Club and Jewish Community in Urban America, 1940–1990.* New York: New York University Press, 1990.

State Secretary of New York State. *Census of Slaves, 1755, vol.3.* New York: State Secretary of New York State, 1850.

Stiles, Henry R. *The Civil, Political, Professional and Ecclesiastical History and Commercial and Industrial Record of the County of Kings and the City of Brooklyn, N.Y. From 1683 to 1884.* New York: W. W. Munsell & Co., 1884.

Sutton, Constance R., and Elsa M. Chaney, eds. *Caribbean Life in New York City: Sociocultural Dimensions.* New York: The Center for Migration Studies of New York, Inc., 1987.

VanDerzee, Charlene, ed. *An Introduction to the Black Contribution to the Development of Brooklyn: A Permanent Exhibition.* Brooklyn: New Muse Community Museum of Brooklyn, 1977.

Van Gelder, Lawrence. *The New York Times*, March 7, 1995.

Vanderbilt, Gertrude Lefferts. *The Social History of Flatbush, and Manners and Customs of the Dutch Settlers in Kings County.* New York: Appleton and Co., 1882.

The Village Voice, August 27, 1988.

Weisman, Steven. "How New York Became a Fiscal Junkie," *The New York Times*, August 17, 1975.

Weld, Ralph Foster. *A Tower on the Heights: The Story of the First Presbyterian Church of Brooklyn.* New York: Columbia University Press, 1946.

———. *Brooklyn Is America.* New York: Columbia University, 1950.

Wilder, Craig Steven. *A Covenant with Color; Race and Social Power in Brooklyn.* New York: Columbia University Press, 1993.

Williams, Eric. *The Negro in the Caribbean.* Howard University and Manchester, UK: Panaf Service Ltd., 1942.

———. *Capitalism and Slavery.* Chapel Hill, NC: The University of North Carolina Press, 1944.

———. *The Negro in the Caribbean.* Manchester, UK: Panaf Service, Ltd., 1945.

Wilson, Sherrill D. *New York City's African Slave Owners: A Social and Material Culture History.* New York: Garland Publishing, Inc., 1994.

Witkin, Richard. *The New York Times,* October 19, 1965.

www.ingramcontent.com/pod-product-compliance
Lightning Source LLC
LaVergne TN
LVHW082338200926
848481LV00012B/3385
* 9 7 8 0 7 5 7 5 9 8 4 0 1 *